TEACHING TECHNIQUES IN ENGLISH AS A SECOND LANGUAGE
Series Editors: Russell N. Campbell and William E. Rutherford

TECHNIQUES IN TESTING

Harold S. Madsen

·OXFORD UNIVERSITY PRESS·

Oxford University Press

200 Madison Avenue
New York, NY 10016 USA

Walton Street
Oxford OX2 6DP England

Library of Congress Cataloging in Publication Data

Madsen, Harold S.
Techniques in testing.

(Teaching techniques in English as a second language)
Includes index.
1. English language–Study and teaching–Foreign speakers. 2. English language–Ability testing.
3. English language–Examinations. I. Title. II. Series.
PE1128.A2M27 1983 428′.007′1 83-8364
ISBN 0-19-434132-1 (pbk.)

First published 1983

Printing (last digit): 10 9 8 7 6

Illustrations by Steven Schindler.

Printed in Hong Kong

Grateful acknowledgment is given for permission to reprint material from the following:

Mary Lawrence, *Writing as a Thinking Process* (Ann Arbor: University of Michigan Press, 1972), p. 85. Copyright © The University of Michigan, 1972.

English for Today, Book 2: The World We Live In, 2nd edition. 1973. Copyright NCTE. Reprinted by permission of the publisher, McGraw-Hill.

Russell Baker, "From Bing to Elvis," *New York Times,* October 18, 1977. © 1977 by the New York Times Company. Reprinted by permission.

Jack Martin, "Everybody's Jogging," adapted by permission from *Nation's Business* Magazine, September 1978.

James M. Hendrickson and Angela Labarca, *The Spice of Life* (New York: Harcourt Brace Jovanovich, Inc., 1979), pp. 99–100. Reprinted by permission of the publisher.

Alexandra Sheedy, "How Can Mom and Dad *Do* This to Me?" *Seventeen*® Magazine, August 1977. Reprinted from *Seventeen*® Magazine. Copyright © 1977 by Triangle Communications, Inc. All rights reserved.

Specified excerpts, abridged and adapted (pp. 30, 64, 73, 194, 234) from *Language and Life in the U.S.A.,* Volume I–Communicating in English, Third Edition, by Gladys G. Doty and Janet Ross. Copyright © 1960 by Harper & Row, Publishers, Inc. Copyright © 1968, 1973 by Gladys G. Doty. Reprinted by permission of the publisher.

Ted Plaister, *Developing Listening Comprehension for ESL Students.* p. 19. © 1976. Reprinted by permission of Prentice-Hall, Inc., Englewood Cliffs, New Jersey.

To Mona,
my parents,
and my children

·EDITORS' PREFACE·

It has been apparent for some time that little attention has been given to the needs of practicing and student teachers of English as a Second Language.* Although numerous inservice and preservice teacher-training programs are offered throughout the world, these often suffer for lack of appropriate instructional materials. Seldom are books written that present practical information that relates directly to daily classroom instruction. What teachers want are useful ideas, suggestions, demonstrations, and examples of teaching techniques that have proven successful in the classroom–techniques that are consistent with established theoretical principles and that others in our profession have found to be expedient, practical, and relevant to the real-life circumstances in which most teachers work.

It was in recognition of this need that we began our search for scholars in our field who had distinguished themselves in particular instructional aspects of second language teaching. We sought out those who had been especially successful in communicating to their colleagues the characteristics of language teaching and testing techniques that have been found to be appropriate for students from elementary school through college and adult education programs. We also sought in those same

*In this volume, and in others in the series, we have chosen to use *English as a Second Language (ESL)* to refer to English teaching in the United States (as a second language) *as well as* English teaching in other countries (as a foreign language).

scholars evidence of an awareness and understanding of current theories of language learning, together with the ability to translate the essence of a theory into practical applications for the classroom.

Our search has been successful. For this volume, as well as for others in this series, we have chosen a colleague who is extraordinarily competent and exceedingly willing to share with practicing teachers the considerable knowledge that he has gained from many years of experience in many parts of the world.

Dr. Madsen's book is devoted entirely to the presentation and exemplification of practical testing techniques. Each chapter of his book contains, in addition to detailed consideration of a wide variety of techniques, a number of activities that teachers can perform that tie the content of the book directly to the teachers' responsibilities in their classes. With this volume then, a critical need in the language teaching field has been met.

We are extremely pleased to join with the authors in this series and with Oxford University Press in making these books available to our fellow teachers. We are confident that the books will enable language teachers around the world to increase their effectiveness while at the same time making their task an easier and more enjoyable one.

Russell N. Campbell
William E. Rutherford

Editors' Note: Apologies are made for the generalized use of the masculine pronoun. It is meant to be used for simplicity's sake, rather than to indicate a philosophical viewpoint. We feel that the *s/he, her/him, his/her* forms, while they may be philosophically appealing, are confusing.

·ACKNOWLEDGMENTS·

I would like to acknowledge the helpful insights from Series editors Russell N. Campbell and William E. Rutherford, the initial encouragement from Marilyn Rosenthal of Oxford University Press, the valuable assistance of editors Debra Sistino and Susan Kulick, the careful reading and excellent suggestions of Randall L. Jones, as well as the useful comments of students in my testing classes.

H.S.M.

·CONTENTS·

TECHNIQUES IN TESTING

·CHAPTER ONE·

INTRODUCTION

Testing is an important part of every teaching and learning experience. This book on testing has been prepared for both experienced and inexperienced teachers of English as a Second Language (ESL) who feel a need to improve their skills in constructing and administering classroom tests at the middle and secondary school levels or in ESL courses for adult students.

We begin in this introductory chapter with a brief look at the history of language testing and then consider the current status of language testing.

In later chapters we provide specific explanations, descriptions, examples, and precautions for the preparation of tests that you and your colleagues might wish to construct as part of your teaching responsibility. In Part I of the book we examine tests of English language features including vocabulary, grammar, and pronunciation tests. In Part II we consider tests of language use including reading, writing, speaking, and listening. The Appendix lists some of the tests used around the world today to measure overall language proficiency such as the Test of English as a Foreign Language (TOEFL) and the Michigan Tests, as well as tests to measure language dominance.

THE IMPORTANCE OF TESTING

How Testing Helps Students Learning English

Well-made tests of English can help students in at least two ways.

First of all, *such tests can help create positive attitudes toward your class.* In the interest of motivation and efficient instruction, teachers almost universally aim at providing positive classroom experiences for their students. There are some important ways that testing can contribute to this aim. One that applies in nearly every class is a sense of accomplishment. In the early 1970s students in an intensive ESL program were being taught from an unstructured conversation-based text. These students complained that while they had ample opportunity to converse in English, they were "not learning anything." Soon afterwards, however, periodic evaluation provided them with a sense of accomplishment that ended their dissatisfaction. Tests of appropriate difficulty, announced well in advance and covering skills scheduled to be evaluated, can also contribute to a positive tone by demonstrating your spirit of fair play and consistency with course objectives.

A second way that English tests can benefit students is by helping them master the language. They are helped, of course, when they study for exams and again when exams are returned and discussed. Where several tests are given, learning can also be enhanced by students' growing awareness of your objectives and the areas of emphasis in the course. Tests can foster learning, too, by their diagnostic characteristics: They confirm what each person has mastered, and they point up those language items needing further attention. Naturally, a better awareness of course objectives and personal language needs can help your students adjust their personal goals. For example, one person might note your strong test emphasis on aural comprehension, and he might also find that he had missed several vocabulary items on a recent test. One logical step would be for him to concentrate on the *meaning* of troublesome words, especially in a spoken context. Learning to spell them or recognize them in a printed context would become a second priority.

In short, properly made English tests can help create *positive attitudes* toward instruction by giving students a sense of accomplishment and a feeling that the teacher's evaluation of them matches what he has taught them. Good English tests also *help students learn the language* by requiring them to study hard, emphasizing course objectives, and showing them where they need to improve.

How Testing Helps Teachers of English

We who teach English as a Second or Foreign Language are generally expected to be accountable for the results of our instruction. Our tests can help us answer the important question "Have I been effective in my teaching?" In other words, we can use them to diagnose our own efforts as well as those of our students. As we record the test scores, we might well ask ourselves the following questions: "Are my lessons on the right level? Or am I aiming my instruction too low or too high?" "Am I teaching some skills effectively but others less effectively?" "What areas do we need more work on? Which points need reviewing?" "Should I spend more (or less) time on this material with next year's students?"

And tests can provide insights into ways that we can improve the evaluation process itself: "Were the test instructions clear?" "Was everyone able to finish in the allotted time?" "Did the test cause unnecessary anxiety or resentment?" "Did the test results reflect accurately how my students have been responding in class and in their assigned work?"

Tests, then, can benefit students, teachers, and even administrators by confirming progress that has been made and showing how we can best redirect our future efforts. In addition, good tests can sustain or enhance class morale and aid learning.

THE STATE OF THE ART IN LANGUAGE TESTING

Recent Historical Trends

Language testing today reflects current interest in teaching genuine communication, but it also reflects earlier concerns for scientifically sound tests. Testing during the last century and the early decades of this one was basically *intuitive*, or subjective and dependent on the personal impressions of teachers. After the intuitive stage, testing entered a *scientific* stage, a time that stressed objective evaluation by language specialists. We are now in a *communicative* stage, a time when we emphasize evaluation of language use rather than language form.

During the long intuitive era, teachers, untrained in testing, evaluated students in a variety of ways. Facts about English often weighed as heavily as skill in using the language. As a result, students had to label parts of a sentence and memorize lists of language patterns (I am, we are, you are, he/she/it is, etc.). Another characteristic of these rather subjective tests was abundant writing in various forms including translation, essay, dictation, précis, and open-ended answers based on reading comprehension. Some of this evaluation was quite sound, especially for advanced students. There was also reliance upon knowledge of grammatical information exemplified by directions such as, "Rewrite the following sentences substituting the present perfect continuous form of the verb."[1]

The scientific era followed the intuitive stage in testing. During the scientific era, many changes occurred. Testing specialists with linguistic training entered the scene. Careful linguistic description suggested that language mastery could be evaluated "scientifically" bit by bit. Objective tests were devised that measured performance or recognition of separate sounds, specific grammatical features, or vocabulary items. These tests often used long lists of unrelated sentences that were incomplete or that contained errors in grammar or usage. Students completed or corrected those sentences by selecting appropriate multiple-choice items. Subjective written tests began to be replaced by objective tests because the latter could be scored consistently even by untrained people. Specialists started to evaluate tests statistically, looking at the effectiveness of each question and measuring the examination's *reliability* and *validity* (see page 178). The new tests and statistical procedures contributed to a growing body of language research. Among the interesting by-products were language aptitude tests, which were designed to predict success in learning a second language.

Tests today are mainly concerned with evaluating real communication in the second language. In this communicative era of testing, we feel that the best exams are those that combine various subskills as we do when exchanging ideas orally or in writing. In particular, communicative tests need to measure more than isolated language skills: They should indicate how well a person can *function* in his second language. Fortunately, in constructing tests today, we don't need to turn our backs on the developments of the scientific period. Earlier, as we recall, there was a movement from rather subjective to highly objective testing. Today's tests tend to use the best features of these two extremes. A relatively new test type, the *cloze,* reflects this compromise: From a story or essay, words are removed at regular intervals (every seventh word, for example). After considering the context, the examinee has to fill in the missing words. Thus, the task is holistic—that is, grammar and vocabulary and overall meaning are tested simultaneously. But the scoring is quite objective.

How exactly do these trends relate to our preparation of classroom tests today? For one thing, we are concerned almost exclusively with measuring skill. *Knowledge* of specific linguistic, literary, or cultural facts may be required in advanced ESL courses, but such information appears only indirectly if at all in our tests of language performance. Good tests can be written without requiring students to use any of the linguistic terminology so common in earlier evaluation. Secondly, certain exam types are now in rather restricted use—for example, translation tests are seldom used nowadays, although they occasionally show up on tests for advanced students, or on specialized tests for translators and on overseas leaving exams where translation is still part of the curriculum. Similarly, précis writing seems generally more appropriate for native speakers or advanced ESL students in an academic setting where the ability to summarize may be important.

Dictation tests, which were criticized during the scientific period, again have rather widespread acceptance. The essay is likewise widely used once more for classroom testing at intermediate and advanced levels. And objective tests are commonplace. Over the years, they have been used to measure all of the language skills. Now, a principal classroom application of objective exams is to evaluate progress in areas such as vocabulary and grammar. Cloze, a relative newcomer in language testing, is already being used around the globe.

Test Classification

We will outline here rather briefly some of the ways tests can be classified. Understanding contrasting exam types can be helpful to teachers since tests of one kind may not always be successfully substituted for those of another kind.

Table 1 · CONTRASTING CATEGORIES OF ESL TESTS

Knowledge Tests	Performance (or Skills) Tests
Subjective Tests	Objective Tests
Productive Tests	Receptive Tests
Language Subskill Tests	Communication Skills Tests
Norm-referenced Tests	Criterion-referenced Tests
Discrete-point Tests	Integrative Tests
Proficiency Tests	Achievement Tests

Let's review the contrasts shown in Table 1. First, tests of *knowledge* are used in various school subjects, from math and geography to literature and language. While ESL knowledge exams show how well students know *facts* about the language, ESL *performance* exams show how well a student can *use* the language. Because today's ESL teachers are concerned with teaching and measuring language skills, this textbook will be concerned only with performance tests.

The second contrast shown in Table 1 is that of *subjective* and *objective* examinations. Subjective tests, like translation and essay, have the advantage of measuring language skill naturally, almost the way English is used in real life. However, many teachers are not able to score such tests quickly and consistently. By contrast, objective exams, such as multiple-choice or matching tests, *can* be scored quickly and consistently.

To continue down the list in Table 1:

Productive measures, like speaking exams, require active or creative answers, while *receptive* measures, like multiple-choice reading tests, tend to rely on recognition, with students simply choosing the letter of the best answer.

Tests of *language subskills* measure the separate components of English, such as vocabulary, grammar, and pronunciation (Chapters 2, 3, and 4 of this book). *Communication skills* tests, on the other hand, show how well students can use the language in actually exchanging ideas and information (Chapters 5 to 8 of this book).

Another set of contrasting tests is that of *norm-referenced* and *criterion-referenced* exams. Norm-referenced tests compare each student with his classmates (most classroom tests are like this). But criterion-referenced exams rate students against certain standards, regardless of how other students do.

Still another pair of categories is that of *discrete-point* and *integrative* tests. In discrete-point exams, each item tests something very specific such as a preposition or a vocabulary item. Integrative tests are those like dictation that combine various language subskills much the way we do when we communicate in real life.

A final classification is *proficiency* and *achievement* tests. Proficiency tests can measure overall mastery of English or how well prepared one is to use English in a particular setting such as an auto mechanics course or a university. Achievement tests, on the other hand, simply measure progress—gains for example in mastery of count-noncount noun use or mastery of the skills presented in an entire language text or course. This book concentrates on how to prepare achievement tests.

It should be apparent from this discussion that several labels can be applied to any one test. But we normally apply only one pair of labels at a time, just as we do in reference to an individual who might simultaneously be a friend, lawyer, wife, mother, and mayor.

Chapters 2, 3, and 4 of this book deal with measuring performance in language subskills. Chapters 5 through 8 cover integrative and communicative skills. The concluding chapter provides ways of evaluating your tests. Techniques for beginners and children are presented at the beginning of each chapter.

Concluding each chapter is an Activities section that allows you to work on those items you need further practice with.

·PART I·

TESTING LANGUAGE SUBSKILLS

Language components involved in communicating include vocabulary, grammar, and pronunciation. While they are all blended in a skill such as listening, it is possible to test how well each component has been mastered individually as a "subskill" of listening or of speaking, for example.

Part I of this book explains how to evaluate mastery of the subskills of English. Of course, tests of language subskills, such as vocabulary, do not show exactly how well a person *uses* English, but they can help teachers diagnose students' strengths and weaknesses in oral or written communication. Chapter 2 explains various ways to test vocabulary mastery; Chapter 3 presents options for examining grammar; and Chapter 4 shows the basic techniques for evaluating pronunciation.

Every chapter contains three or four sections, each one describing a different kind of testing technique. The first section presents ways to test beginning language learners of any age. Skill in *preparing* various kinds of exam questions is developed through the Activities section that concludes each chapter.

Choosing which kind of vocabulary, grammar, or pronunciation test to use depends on the students' age and language ability as well as on the kind of skill being taught, such as speaking or reading. Results from subskill tests can point out which matters need special attention in the classroom.

· CHAPTER TWO ·

VOCABULARY TESTS

The purpose of vocabulary tests is to measure the comprehension and production of words used in speaking or writing. After a brief discussion of *what* words to test, the balance of the chapter will illustrate *how* to evaluate vocabulary mastery.

Four general kinds of vocabulary tests are presented. The first, limited response, is for beginners. These test items require either a simple physical action like pointing at something or a very simple verbal answer such as "yes" or "no." The second, multiple-choice completion, is a test in which a sentence with a missing word is presented; students choose one of four vocabulary items given to complete the sentence. A third type, multiple-choice paraphrase, is a test in which a sentence with one word underlined is given. Students choose which of four words is the closest in meaning to the underlined item. A fourth kind of test, simple completion (words), has students write in the missing part of words that appear in sentences. Concluding the discussion of each test type you will find a summary of the advantages and limitations of the test type presented. The discussion of test types 2, 3, and 4 also includes a list of alternate forms of the technique being described.

Simply choosing difficult words or random lists of words doesn't make much sense. Somehow we need to find out which words our students need to know. Occasionally the problem is solved by a course syllabus that tells what words must be learned. In some countries, subjects like mathematics and history are taught in English at upper levels. In this situation, you can ask the mathematics teacher, for example, to provide technical words and phrases that need to be mastered for his course. Another way is to record the words that students misuse. These become test items. Still other sources are your textbook, reader, and exercise manual. Finally, do not overlook the words and phrases needed to run the class, such as "Take your seat" or "the assignment for tomorrow." These are useful test items at the beginning level.

Deciding how to test vocabulary is related to how we teach it. Most ESL teachers today do not recommend having students simply memorize lists of words. Instead, they teach students to find the meaning of words through the context of the sentence, and they help increase comprehension by teaching important affixes (happy: **un**happy/beauty: beauti**ful**). In *testing* vocabulary, we also need to avoid presenting words in isolation. This chapter will illustrate a variety of ways to use context cues and word-building skills in testing vocabulary.

Checking vocabulary mastery can be adjusted to match your emphasis on oral or written skills. Suppose improving conversation skills is your primary objective: You can test vocabulary by using aural cues ("What time is it?") and by requiring spoken answers ("It's nine o'clock"). On the other hand, suppose you are stressing reading: You can offer a written multiple-choice format ("He bought a cake at the (A) bank, (B) bakery, (C) hardware store, (D) bookstore").

And let's not overlook informal evaluation, which can be useful in measuring any language skill. One example of such evaluation is homework exercises; another is classroom practice. This can even include game-type activities such as crossword puzzles and "Twenty Questions." In playing "Twenty Questions," students try to identify an object by asking yes-no questions; to win, they must identify it within twenty guesses. ("Students, something from my desk is in the box. Ask me what it is. I will answer only yes or no."/"Is it your ruler?" . . .) Even vocabulary *exercises* can be used as progress tests. Because students are familiar with such exercises, test anxiety can be reduced.

LIMITED RESPONSE

In testing children and beginning-level adults, we often use directed physical responses and visuals. We do this to avoid language skills that have not been mastered yet. For these tests, students don't have to know how to read or write. In fact, they don't even have to know how to speak.

Individual Testing

Directed physical responses can easily be used when you test one student at a time. When elementary school students are taught to read, their teachers generally arrange for small-group activity and individual work. Individual interaction can also be very productive *when testing language skills* of beginning students. A surprising amount of information can be gathered in just two to three minutes. After basic commands have been learned (such as "Go to the . . ." and "Hand me the . . ."), you can check mastery of certain vocabulary by saying, "Please go to the window" or "Please hand me the chalk." The student can show he understands by doing what he is told.

In addition, you can test beginning students by asking for only a very short answer—for example, "Is the book green?" There are of course other kinds of brief answers that can be used with visuals ("What color is the book?"/"Green" or "Is the boy sleeping or swimming?"/"[He's] swimming").

Group Testing

You can use nonverbal physical responses as well to test the whole class at the same time. A good way is to draw or duplicate a sketch such as the one on the opposite page and give one to each person in the class. After an example (such as, "Draw a circle around the boy"), you can say, "Now draw a circle around a tree." Another command might be to "Put an 'X' on every tool." Still another would be to have an empty clock face on the paper. You could then have students draw hands on the clock showing, for example, that it is 3:30. Another task would be to

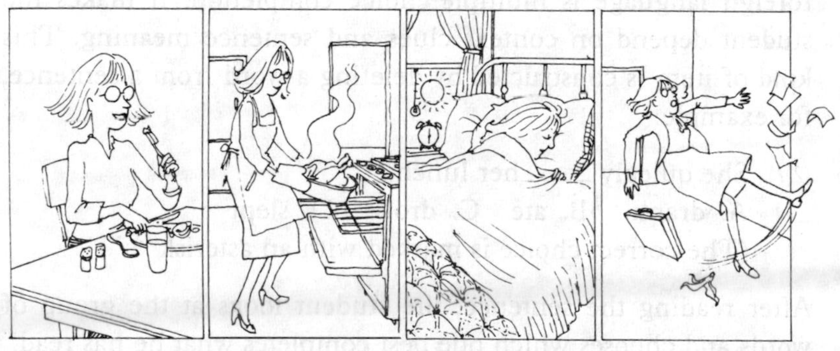

duplicate for them a set of pictures such as the one above. Then have them circle the activity that matches your sentence ("My friend is eating").

Naturally, activities, visuals, and objects can be used with more advanced students as well: A botany student could name the parts of a flower, and a technical student could describe a pump. But we normally use other ways to test people who can read and write.

Advantages of Limited Response

1. It causes less stress or nervousness than other types of tests.
2. It avoids skills such as reading and writing that have not yet been developed.
3. It can be scored easily and objectively.

Limitations of Limited Response

1. It requires individual testing, which takes longer than group testing.
2. It is usually difficult to test abstract words with this technique.
3. Sketches are sometimes ambiguous (e.g., an orange may look like a ball; running may look like dancing or jumping).

MULTIPLE-CHOICE COMPLETION

A good vocabulary test type for students who can read in the foreign language is multiple-choice completion. It makes the student depend on context clues and sentence meaning. This kind of item is constructed by deleting a word from a sentence, for example:

(2.1) She quickly _____ her lunch.
A. drank *B. ate C. drove D. slept
(The correct choice is marked with an asterisk"*.")

After reading the sentence, the student looks at the group of words and chooses which one best completes what he has read.

The following steps should be taken in writing multiple-choice completion items: (1) Select the words to be tested. (2) Get the right kind of sentence to put each word in (this sentence context is called the *stem*). (3) Choose several wrong words to put the right word with (these wrong words are called *distractors*). Three distractors plus the right word are enough for a written item. (4) Finally, prepare clear and simple instructions. And if this kind of test question is new to your students, it would be good to prepare one or two examples. In the paragraphs that follow, we will discuss each of these matters.

Vocabulary Choice

When selecting vocabulary items, remember the suggestions given earlier in the chapter. Also, realize that sentence-completion items give you a chance to test passive vocabulary. Since students have to recognize these words but not necessarily produce them, this is a good way to test more difficult vocabulary items. But these should still be words or phrases that are useful to your students—words, for example, from their reading materials. Of course, words can be chosen from other sources like newspapers, magazines, and textbooks from other classes, if you have used these in your English class. Another point to remember is that usually only content words (nouns, verbs, adjectives, and adverbs) are included in vocabulary tests. Function words (articles, determiners, prepositions, conjunctions, pronouns, auxiliary verbs) appear in grammar tests.

When using words not found in your ESL class text, be careful of bias. Material from a business or secretarial class could give students who attend these classes a special advantage (most students may not know specialized words like **debit, account, balance, margin, erase, file**). Cultural bias can also be a problem for those not familiar, for example, with Western or American ways and expressions: **laundromat** [a commercial self-service laundry], **sunny side up** [an egg fried on only one side], **three credit hours** [typically, three periods of college instruction per week]. There is even a possibility of sex bias (which of the following words would male students be less likely to know than female students: **recipe, carburetor, hosiery, screwdriver?**).

Context Preparation

With suitable words selected, our next step is to prepare contexts for them. Sometimes—especially for beginning students—more than one sentence is needed to help clarify meaning. You can prepare a two-line mini-dialog like those in the students' books, to check the meaning of a word such as (paint)**brush:**

(2.2) "I want to paint, too."
"All right. Use that _____ over there."
*A. brush B. pencil C. broom D. spoon

Another way is to find a passage (on your students' level) in which the word appears, remembering that some sentences are much more helpful than others. Consider a fairly difficult word—**communicate.** A passage from an ESL reader might begin with the sentence: "Human beings **communicate** in many ways." This shows us only that **communicate** is a verb and that it can be performed by humans. Another sentence from the same passage limits the meaning of the word: "Some people **communicate** disapproval by holding their nose between their thumb and forefinger." This second sentence provides a better "frame" for the word. Other verbs such as **interrogate, philosophize,** and **investigate** can be used as distractors with the second sentence. (Again, an asterisk indicates the correct answer.)

(2.3) Some people ____ disapproval by holding their nose between their thumb and forefinger.
A. interrogate B. philosophize *C. communicate
D. investigate

A, B, and D are good distractors because not one of them fits this context.

Assume that a second rather difficult word, **superstitious,** appears only in a general context: "Frank is certainly very **superstitious.**" We see that a large number of words (such as **old, tall, happy, kind;** or **ambitious, optimistic, courteous**) could fit here. Since a better sentence is not available in the text, we can write one of our own: "Frank is so **superstitious** that he thinks you'll have bad luck if you break a mirror." Simplified slightly, it reads:

(2.4) Frank is very ____; he says, "Break a mirror, and you'll have bad luck."
A. ambitious B. optimistic C. courteous
*D. superstitious

Finally, avoid contexts that are too difficult. The following sentence contextualizes the verb **implies,** which you may want to test, but notice how difficult it is to understand: "Present an analogy which **implies** the concept you wish to convey." The vocabulary item is much more easily understood in the following context: "He didn't actually say so, but he **implied** that you lied."

Distractor Preparation

There are two common ways to choose distractors. Experienced teachers often create their own. They can do so because they have developed a "feel" for the language that is appropriate for their students. But there is a second and equally good way. That is to use student errors as distractors.

Teachers who create their own distractors should follow certain guidelines:

1. Make sure the distractors are the same form of word as the correct answer. (Here and elsewhere in this book, the word "poor" indicates that there is something bad about the sample test item and that it should be avoided.)

(2.5) **(poor)** She had to help the ____ old man up the stairs.

*A. weak B. slowly C. try D. wisdom

When distractors are not the same form as the right answer, students might answer the item correctly for the wrong reason. For example, some may know an adjective is needed in item 2.5 and they might notice that **weak** is the only adjective listed. (Note that words like **strong, energetic,** and **athletic** are distractors that contrast with the old man's weakened condition. On the other hand, words such as **wise, kind, pleasant,** and **bent** do not contrast as well and are therefore weaker distractors.)

2. Also be sure you don't give away the right answer through grammatical cues. Notice the effect of the article in the following example.

(2.6) **(poor)** She needs to get up earlier so she's buying an ____ clock.

A. time *B. alarm C. watch D. bell

In this question, meaning *and* grammar indicate that **alarm clock** is right because **an** is only used with a word beginning with a vowel sound. One way of correcting this would be to remove **an** from the sentence and use this form for the choices: A. a time ★B. an alarm C. a watch D. a bell.

3. Multiple-choice items for any one question should be about the same level of difficulty, and ideally, the sentence context should not be difficult for students to read.

(2.7) **(poor)** They needed lots of training to operate such ____ equipment.
A. easy ★B. sophisticated C. blue D. wise

Students might pick **sophisticated** simply because it contrasts in difficulty with the distractors or because students can eliminate the three easy choices.

4. Also be sure not to include more than one correct answer.

(2.8) **(poor)** She sent the ____ yesterday.
★A. letter B. gift C. food D. books

Actually, any one of the four choices is acceptable. The item would be improved by changing the verb to **mailed.** But we know that gifts, food, and books are also mailed. Therefore, we can use *unmailable* choices such as **post office, friend,** or **courage.** Another possibility is to choose a new sentence. But notice how this problem can arise again:

(2.9) **(poor)** She wrote a ____ yesterday.
★A. letter B. gift C. friend D. book

While "D" is unlikely, "C" is completely acceptable. So we still have two "correct" answers, and of course we should have only one. To eliminate slips like these, have someone else read through your items before you use them on a test.

At the beginning of the discussion on distractors it was suggested that you could write your own, or that you could use student errors. One source of student errors is the composition, and another is student speech. These are good because they involve actual communication. The difficulty is that such sources take a lot of time to sort through, and usually much of the information that we want is missing, because students can avoid words that they are not sure of.

A more efficient way to find vocabulary errors is to look at homework and classroom exercises on vocabulary. But if the test that you're preparing is important enough, you can collect errors (for distractors) even more systematically: Give the students sentence-completion items without the multiple-choice options, and simply have them fill in the blank in each sentence. You can then write down their wrong answers. You will also find some correct alternatives, but naturally you can't use these as distractors. For example, suppose you used "Frank is very . . . ; he says, 'Break a mirror, and you'll have bad luck.'" Besides **superstitious,** you might get words such as **silly, wrong, stupid, liar, because, religious, knowing, lucky.** The first three can't be used because they could possibly appear in such a sentence. The last three are adjectives, and so they seem usable. However, **liar** and **because** do not match distractor requirements. What do you do with these? You can probably use them anyway, particularly if more than one person wrote them down. Our guidelines are useful generalizations, but the errors made by your students reflect their exact level and their special way of "seeing" the language. Distractors chosen from these errors can test your class even better than those that you create yourself.

Instruction Preparation

The instructions for your test should be brief; students shouldn't have to spend a lot of time reading them. And they should be clear; anxiety can come from poorly worded questions, and resentment from misunderstood directions. Some teachers prefer to give instructions orally, but if any students come late, repeated instructions can distract those working on the exam. Keep in mind that instructions can really become a kind of "test," and oral instructions can amount to an unintended "listening test."

If you have used multiple-choice sentence-completion exercises in class, instructions can be very short: "Circle the letter of the right answers" (or) "Circle the letter of the word that best completes each sentence." Naturally the kind of directions given depends on your students' reading ability and how you want them to mark the test paper. Consider the following:

Read each sentence carefully. Then look at the four

words below it. Choose the one that completes the sentence correctly. Put the letter of that word (A, B, C, or D) in the blank at the left.

You will find it helpful to give both oral and written instructions for students at the beginning level. For classes with the same language background and with very little skill in English, you can even give the instructions in the native language.

One final note: Instructions can be made more clear by one or two examples. They are not given primarily for practice. They are given to show how to answer the questions. Therefore, they should be simple enough that everyone can do them without any difficulty.

(2.10) *Example:* They drove to work in their new ____.
A. house *B. car C. office D. street

If needed, a short explanation can follow the example: "We circle 'B' because 'car' is the only word that fits into the sentence."

Alternate Forms of Multiple-Choice Completion

Following are alternate ways to prepare vocabulary multiple-choice completion items:

1. Definition.

(2.11) To ____ someone means to save him or her from danger.
A. praise B. injure *C. rescue D. announce

2. Phrase completion.

a. Idioms.

(2.12) The committee____ choosing you as president.
*A. wound up B. buttoned down C. wiped out D. sat in

b. Appropriateness to context.

(2.13) The newspaper says, "A two-year-old girl ____ today when struck by a bus."

A. kicked the bucket B. was eradicated *C. was killed D. departed

3. Phrasal context (not *sentence* completion).

(2.14) _____ his fingernails
A. tailored B. reduced C. remodeled
*D. manicured

4. Multiple-choice cloze. (Cloze tests are discussed in Chapter 3.) Cloze tests are made from stories or essays by deleting words at regular intervals. Students have to write in each blank the word that they think belongs there. Multiple-choice cloze tests work like regular multiple-choice sentence completion; but usually content words (like **school** or **run**) *and* function words (such as **the** or **in**) are deleted. In addition, cloze tests provide more context–often more than one paragraph. Multiple-choice cloze can test vocabulary when only content words are deleted.

(2.15) After the capture of Troy, Ulysses set out for his
(A. neighborhood B. continent *C. homeland
D. street) many miles away. But so many strange
(A. sights *B. things C. places D. people) happened to him on his journey that ten
(*A. years B. times C. roads D. cities) passed
before he reached Ithaca![1]

Advantages of Multiple-Choice Completion

1. It helps students see the full meaning of words by providing natural contexts. Also, it is a good influence on instruction: It discourages word-list memorization.
2. Scoring is easy and consistent.
3. It is a sensitive measure of achievement.

Limitations of Multiple-Choice Completion

1. It is rather difficult to prepare good sentence contexts that clearly show the meaning of the word being tested.
2. It is easy for students to cheat by copying what others have circled.

MULTIPLE-CHOICE PARAPHRASE

Multiple-choice paraphrase tests of vocabulary items offer much of the same advantage that multiple-choice completion tests do, and the contexts are much easier to prepare. Understanding is checked by the student's having to choose the best synonym or paraphrase of the vocabulary item. A sentence context is still used. However, choosing the right word depends more on knowing the key vocabulary item than on finding meaning in the sentence. In fact, the context may simply show that the item is a noun.

Vocabulary Choice and Context Preparation

In writing paraphrase items, we follow the same steps that we took to prepare completion items: (1) Select the words to be tested; (2) prepare a sentence context; (3) choose distractors; and (4) write instructions. Choose words just as you did in the last section, but you can spend less effort in preparing sentence contexts. Now the meaning comes more from the emphasized word than from its context. Here is a typical item:

(2.16) He was **irate** when he heard about the new plans.
A. interested B. surprised *C. angry D. sad

But students with very little English won't know synonyms for very many words. Also there are some words in their ESL books that are difficult to find equivalents for. Consider the word **pilot,** for example, which appears in a number of elementary ESL texts. It can be tested by explaining the meaning:

(2.17) My sister is a **pilot.** She can ____.
A. help sick people B. make clothes *C. fly an airplane D. teach students at school

Distractor Preparation

In preparing one-word distractors, keep in mind the suggestions made in the section on multiple-choice completion. In addition, here are some guidelines that apply particularly (though not exclusively) to paraphrase items.

1. Try to get distractors that are related to the subject covered in the sentence. This is particularly true in testing intermediate and advanced students.

(2.18) **(poor)** He just hit his **shin.**
★A. leg B. cousin C. fender D. fruit

In reading this, students may recognize **shin** as some part of the body. If so, they can get the question right by the process of elimination. More challenging distractors would include **back, foot,** and **arm.**

2. Try to avoid pairing a word of opposite meaning with the right answer. Often this attracts students and gives them a better chance of getting the item right.

(2.19) **(poor)** He plans to **purchase** some candy for his mother.
A. make ★B. buy C. sell D. steal

3. Try to avoid using distractors with the same meaning. This problem is illustrated in the following example:

(2.20) **(poor)** His **remorse** was great indeed.
A. wealth ★B. sadness C. strength D. power

By accident, new test writers sometimes include two or more distractors that are close in meaning. If the student recognizes this, he can eliminate both, for he knows that only one answer can be right. Since **strength** and **power** are rather close in meaning, the student might decide to choose one of the first two. On the advanced level, however, distractors can be rather close in meaning to the correct answer.

4. Also avoid trick items that use close spelling or sound contrasts, since a vocabulary test is not a spelling exam. Students with limited ability may know the meaning of a word without being certain of its spelling or exact pronunciation.

(2.21) **(poor)** They crossed the ocean on a **liner.**
A. sheep B. streamer C. bolt ★D. vessel

In the example above, the distractors are chosen to sound like ship, steamer, and boat.

5. When using phrase distractors, be careful that the correct answer is not generally the longest. Teachers often make the right answer longer because they want to be sure they have paraphrased the key word adequately.

(2.22) **(poor)** That boy is very unusual; he's a **genius.**
A. can see the future B. has received much money ★C. has unusual mental, inventive, and creative ability D. has a terrible illness

There are two final observations that should be made about writing distractors: First, the multiple-choice items should normally be easier than the key word in the stem. (Consider example 2.16: **Irate** was the key word: **angry** was the answer, and **interested, surprised,** and **sad** were the distractors—all rather easy words.) Second, remember that student errors can be used as distractors. When you use these, you do not have to follow the guidelines we have discussed.

Instruction Preparation

Instructions for multiple-choice paraphrase items can be prepared by following the guidelines for multiple-choice completion instructions in the previous section of this chapter.

Alternate Forms of Multiple-Choice Paraphrase

There are two kinds of paraphrase questions: Both use a key word in a sentence. But one asks the student to find the best synonym or related word, and the other has the student choose the phrase that is the best short definition or paraphrase of the key word. The following are four alternate ways to write paraphrase items.

1. Idioms and other phrases.

(2.23) The salesman seemed quite **down and out.**
★A. poor B. disappointed C. lost D. angry

2. Phrasal context.

(2.24) a **considerate** little lady
A. worried B. tired C. happy *D. kind

3. Reading passage context. (Vocabulary questions can be included with reading comprehension questions.)

Just then we saw him run out of the side door. As he turned the corner, a slip of paper fluttered to the ground. . . . With that paper, the police were able to **trace** the man's whereabouts.

(2.25) In this passage, **trace** means ____.
A. copy B. enter *C. locate D. eliminate

4. Related-word identification. (These questions do not use synonyms; they use examples and nonexamples of the key word.)

(2.26) He eats lots of **vegetables.**
A. bananas B. peaches C. oranges *D. carrots

5. Unrelated-word identification.

(2.27) He lives in a big **house.**
A. attic *B. car C. basement D. bedroom

Advantages of Multiple-Choice Paraphrase

1. Context preparation is rather easy.
2. Scoring is easy and consistent.
3. It is a sensitive measure of achievement.

Limitations of Multiple-Choice Paraphrase

1. It is difficult to find good synonyms (but recall the "explanation" alternative: item 2.17).
2. It is easy for students to cheat.

SIMPLE COMPLETION (WORDS)

Word-formation items require students to fill in missing parts of words that appear in sentences. These missing parts are usually prefixes and suffixes–for example, the **un-** in **untie** or the **-ful** in **thankful.** A related task is to use words like the following in a sentence and have students supply missing syllables of any kind, such as the **rel-** in **relative** or the **-ate** in **deliberate.** We can see, then, that there is a different emphasis in simple-completion tests than in those we have just looked at. Context is still useful, but the emphasis is on word building. Moreover, this is a test of active not passive skills.

The steps in preparing a simple-completion vocabulary test are similar to those followed in the two previous sections, but with one difference: Now no distractors are needed. Here are the steps: (1) List the prefixes and suffixes that you have taught to your students. Then match these with content words that they have studied (including even their passive vocabulary). (2) Prepare sentences that clarify the meaning of these words. (3) Then write your instructions and examples.

If the test is quite important, try it out ahead of time. You can have other teachers take it, or possibly native English speakers. Then revise it and use it in your class.

Vocabulary Choice

Perhaps your students have studied the **-ly** ending used with many adverbs (and some adjectives). They might not know adjectives like **manly** or adverbs like **extremely.** But **quick** is part of their vocabulary, and so it can be used in testing the suffix (quick**ly**). They might also know the negative prefix **un-.** Recalling that **cooperative** is part of their passive vocabulary, you decide to challenge them on the test. You will see if they can produce **uncooperative.**

Context Preparation

Student success on the exam will depend in part on your sentence contexts. For example, one simple-completion vocabulary test included a stem (base word) requiring **-ous.** The sentence read, "He was a very nerv_____ person." But a number of these rather advanced students wrote in a "y" instead–an unexpected but correct ending. They thus produced **nervy,** which means "bold" or "offensive." The context did not show that the person intended was "worried" or "timid" **(nervous),** so **nervy** had to be accepted.

It is also possible to check student knowledge of when *not* to add a prefix or suffix. Compare the following:

(2.28) 1. My teach_____ is very helpful.
(2.29) 2. Did she teach_____ you anything?

In the first sentence, the suffix **-er** is required. In the second sentence, no suffix is needed. Such sentences are not left empty; students must put an "X" in the blank. But notice again how careful we must be in writing our sentences:

(2.30) **(poor)** That was a care_____ answer.

Note that either **careful** or **careless** can be used. Sometimes more context is needed to clarify which word we mean:

(2.31) Yesterday he got on the wrong bus. So today he was care_____ to find the right one.

Instruction Preparation

Instructions, as we have seen, can vary quite a bit. If simple-completion exercises have been used in class, we might give the following directions: "Complete the words in these sentences. When nothing is needed, put an 'X' in the blank." If the simple-completion test is new, we might have something like this:

> Read these sentences carefully. Most have a word that needs to be completed. Write in the part that is missing. Some words do not need anything added. When you find such a word, put an "X" in the blank. Blanks left empty will be marked wrong.

It would be helpful to put examples on the exam for students who have not done simple-completion items before. You would probably need to illustrate a prefix, a suffix, and an "X" blank.

Alternate Forms of Simple-Completion Items

Here are four additional ways to prepare simple-completion questions:

1. Stem-first procedure. (An advantage is that many words need spelling changes when suffixes are added. This allows for such changes.)

(2.32) **(beauty)** She has a beautiful new dress.

2. Phrasal context. (Note that grammatical clues are sometimes given to less advanced students.)

(2.33) an in convenient delay

3. Compounds.

(2.34) He found the bedroom, but he couldn't open the door to the clothes closet.

4. Inflectional cloze. (Cloze tests, as we have said, are discussed in Chapter 3. Or see the short discussion under "Alternate Forms of Multiple-Choice Completion Items" in this chapter.)

(2.35) Every motorist will tell you that radar is used most un fairly by the police to catch drivers who are accidental ly going a little fast er than the speed limit. "There you are," the motorist will say, "driv ing quite safely at 60 on a wide x open road almost in open country. Then a highway patrolman stops you for breaking the speed limit."

Advantages of Simple Completion (Words)

1. It reflects teaching approaches.
2. It is generally faster and easier to construct than are items with distractors.

Limitations of Simple Completion (Words)

1. Fewer words can be tested this way than with multiple choice.
2. There is some difficulty in avoiding ambiguous contexts (see 2.30).

· ACTIVITIES ·

A. LIMITED RESPONSE. (See pages 14 to 16.)

1. Write out five commands that a student can perform (individually) by moving about the room, and five commands that he can perform while sitting down.

2. Write out five commands or questions that a student can respond to (individually) by pointing to a picture that you have found. Include the picture.

3. Using the picture from activity 2, prepare five requests that require students to follow instructions by drawing.

4. Using original line drawings or pictures (from your students' text) showing activities, prepare five vocabulary questions that require short answers. Supply sample answers.

B. MULTIPLE-CHOICE COMPLETION. (See pages 16 to 23.)

1. The following sentences contain examples of distractor difficulties. Identify the weakness in each item. Then correct it. (See item 2.7.)

a. Do you need some _____ to write on?
*A. paper B. pen C. table D. material

b. The mouse_____ quickly away.
A. very B. little C. baby *D. ran

c. I think he'll be here in an _____.
*A. hour B. soon C. weekend D. day after tomorrow

d. They ____ me to get up right away.
A. asked B. needed *C. told D. wanted

2. Prepare five test items from words in your students' text, or use the following vocabulary words: **truth/weekend/secret/ridiculous/perfume.**

a. For each word write a sentence context that reflects the meaning of the word as clearly as possible.
b. Prepare three good distractors for each test item.
c. Write simple, clear instructions, and include an example.

C. MULTIPLE-CHOICE PARAPHRASE. (See pages 24 to 27.)
1. The following items contain examples of distractor difficulties. Identify the weakness in each item. Then correct it.

a. They told us about the **savory** meal that they had just eaten.
A. broken *B. tasty C. unhappy D. helpless
b. What would be the most **convenient** time to come?
*A. easy to do or a comfortable plan for someone
B. happy or beautiful C. close to now D. first in the day
c. He sat down by the **comely** girl.
A. intelligent B. small C. ugly *D. pretty
d. She is a person of good **judgment** and courage.
A. since B. cents C. scents *D. sense

2. Select two verbs, two nouns, and one adverb at the level of your students–if possible from your students' text.

a. Provide an appropriate sentence context for each.
b. Prepare a suitable equivalent word and three distractors for each item.

3. Look at the following items (1–4) which contain student errors.

a. Underline the word that is used improperly.
b. Provide the correct word.

1. Why is that little dog honking at me?
2. Should I shut the light on?
3. She has many differing friends.
4. After I sang, the audience gave me a big handclasp.

D. SIMPLE COMPLETION (WORDS). (See pages 27 to 30.) First, supply a word with a prefix or suffix for each blank in the following sentences. Then prepare simple-completion items.

Example: It was a most _____ mistake.
(*Answer:* deplorable [regrettable, inexcusable, etc.]
It was a most deplor_____ mistake)

1. When you write your check, make it _____ to my sister.
2. Please wipe your _____ hands on that cloth.
3. The police arrested him for _____ the riot.
4. The _____ of the volcano destroyed several villages.
5. The boy didn't _____ his shoelaces before taking off his shoes.

ANSWER KEY

B1

a. more than 1 right answer; b. nonverbs used; c. "an" cues answer; d. more than 1 right answer

C1

a. distractors unrelated to food; b. correct answer is long; c. C and D are opposites; d. spelling trap

C3

1. *honking:* barking; 2. *shut:* turn; 3. *differing:* different; 4. *handclasp:* hand

D

1. pay*able*; 2. dirt*y*; 3. incit*ing*; 4. erupt*ion*;
5. *un*tie

·CHAPTER THREE·

GRAMMAR TESTS

Grammar tests are designed to measure student proficiency in matters ranging from inflections (bottle–bottles, bake–baked) to syntax. Syntax involves the relationship of words in a sentence, including matters such as word order, use of the negative, question forms, and connectives. Each of the four sections of this chapter covers a different approach to testing grammar. The first section, limited response, is especially useful for students at the beginning level. The remaining sections discuss multiple-choice completion, simple completion, and cloze tests.

As indicated earlier, Part I of this book covers vocabulary, grammar, and pronunciation exams. Of these three, grammar tests seem to be the most popular. There are several reasons for this: Much ESL teaching has been based on grammar; and unlike various measures of communicative skills, there is general agreement on what to test. Grammar items, such as auxiliary verbs, are easy to identify, and errors in grammar can be quickly spotted and counted. As with vocabulary exams, either passive or active skills can be checked. Also, grammar can be tailored to beginners or advanced learners.

Of course, in testing grammar, we don't pretend to measure actual communication. But we can do a good job of measuring progress in a grammar class, and we can diagnose student needs in this area.

LIMITED RESPONSE

The grammar of students with very little ability in English can be checked without having them speak or write anything. This can be done by means of directed physical responses and visuals. This section presents two basic ways to measure the grammar skills of these beginning-level students: (1) testing them one at a time, and (2) testing them in groups.

Individual Testing

You can test students individually by using oral requests. These requests can ask for easy spoken replies or simply for nonverbal actions. When teaching students who know almost no English, you can even permit answers in their native language.

> *Example: (students hear in English)*
> "How many books are on the table?"
> *(students answer in their language)*
> "[There are] six."

Remember, of course, to use familiar vocabulary in your test questions as well as structures that students have been taught. For example, you may want to test understanding of the preposition **between;** so you tell a student to "Put the red folder between the two green ones." But if he doesn't know what a **folder** is or what the command **put** means, he will miss the question—even though he knows the preposition. When the numbers, colors, and familiar classroom objects are learned, then you can test, for instance, wh-questions confidently. You might ask, "Where are the three yellow notebooks?" or "Which two pens are red?" The beginning student can answer simply by touching or pointing to the objects.

Pictures like the one on the next page can be used to test students individually or in groups. To test preposition recognition, we can ask, "Is the lady on the house?" Or we can say, "Point to the child behind the car."

Pictures can also be used to test other matters such as verb tense: If students can tell time, clock faces can show when each of a series of activities took place (for example, sketches of a man eating lunch at noon, working at 2:00 p.m., and driving home at

5:30 p.m.). The past tense can be evaluated by asking, "What did he do before he went back to work?"

The picture on page 36 can also be used with more challenging questions; for example, (checking present progressive) "What is the lady doing?" (or checking the conditional) "What would happen if she dropped the can of paint?" (Several correct answers are possible.)

Group Testing

You can also test students in *groups* by using directed physical responses. The following "drawing" activity can test prepositions of place: First, explain and illustrate any new vocabulary words. Then have students make a drawing according to your spoken instructions: "Draw an airplane in the middle of the paper. [*Pause while students draw.*] Now draw a house below the airplane. [*Pause.*] Next draw a cloud in front of the airplane."

Using a picture like the first one in this chapter, you can test your students' understanding of prepositions. For example, we can say, "Draw a circle around the person on the house" or "Draw an 'X' on the boy behind the car." Sets of three or four related pictures can evaluate mastery of a number of grammar points. Here is a set that tests the comparative:

(nonverbal)	"Circle the picture that illustrates this sentence: 'The boy is as big as the girl.'"
(yes-no)	"Look at picture 'B.' Is the boy as big as the girl?"
(true-false)	"Look at picture 'C.' The girl is taller than the boy."

Normally we would use only one type of question on a test—all yes-no or all true-false, for example.

Advantages of Limited Response

1. It puts students at ease and avoids unnecessary stress.
2. It avoids skills such as reading and writing that have not yet been developed.
3. It can be scored easily and objectively.

Limitations of Limited Response

1. Individual testing takes longer than group testing.
2. It is difficult to find suitable pictures (although the teacher can make needed sketches).
3. Only a limited number of grammatical structures can be tested.

MULTIPLE-CHOICE COMPLETION

The test type presented in this section includes an incomplete sentence stem followed by four multiple-choice options for completing the sentence. Here is an easy sample item:

(3.1) She is ____ her breakfast.
⋆A. eating B. ate C. eats D. eaten

While multiple-choice completion is an efficient way to test grammar, teachers need to be cautioned about the temptation to use this kind of item for all of their testing needs. Many people are very excited about objective tests, feeling that multiple-choice objective exams in particular should be used to test everything. However, any given test is a kind of tool; it may be very useful for some jobs but not for others. For example, while multiple-choice tests can be used successfully in testing grammar, they don't seem to work as well in testing conversational ability.

Preparing multiple-choice completion *grammar* items follows about the same procedure as that described in Chapter 2 for writing multiple-choice completion *vocabulary* items: (1) Choose the grammar points that you need to test; (2) prepare the right kind of sentence context (or stem) for the grammar structure; (3) select three logical distractors; and (4) prepare clear, simple instructions.

Grammar Choice

Choosing grammar points to test is usually rather easy: Just determine what structures you have taught since the last test. The results on quizzes or homework assignments can show those things that students have learned well and those things that need reviewing. The points they know well can be largely ignored. A few of these, however, could be included at the beginning of the test to encourage students.

A related matter is how to give different "weight" to various grammar points. Let's say you spent three times longer on modal auxiliaries than on two-word verbs. You could prepare two or three times as many questions on the modals. This is part of the planning that is necessary. Before starting to write the questions, you need to decide how many of each grammar type to include.

Context Preparation

Let's assume that you have decided what points to test, what multiple-choice type to use, and how many questions to prepare. You are now ready to start writing the items. First, choose a structure and then use it correctly in a sentence. Remember, *a good context is very important!* Sometimes only a few words are enough, such as "I don't want **to** go" (in testing "to plus verb"). But notice how much context is needed for other grammar points. In the following sentence, **must** is used to express a conclusion or deduction: "Jimmy hasn't eaten anything, and he won't talk or play. He **must** be ill." When many of your test items require a lot of context like this, you will want to use a two-sentence approach. The two-sentence item above has the same speaker saying both sentences.

Distractor Preparation

We are now ready for distractors. You will recall that these are the incorrect options which we put with the correct word or phrase to complete the sentence. Experienced teachers usually have a good sense for what to use, but inexperienced teachers need some help. For example, "could of" has sometimes been used as a distractor for "could have." This won't work, because it is a native English-speaker error and is almost never made by non-native English speakers. Also, avoid using distractors that sound alike. Look at this item from an inexperienced teacher's test:

(3.2) **(poor)** ____ the ones who know the answers.
*A. They are B. There C. They're D. Their

This is really just a spelling item. It might be used on a writing test, but not on a grammar test. Another problem is that both A and C are correct options.

It is also a good idea to avoid items that test divided usage, or items that only test different levels of formality.

(3.3) **(poor)** You can get it from the lady ____ he sold it to.
A. which B. who *C. whom D. why

Debatable items like this just confuse non-native speakers. Notice that choice "C" is in the "correct" case. But choice "B" is closer to what native speakers would actually say. The easiest way of saying the sentence isn't even provided–dropping out the relative pronoun altogether ("You can get it from the lady he sold it to"). In addition, the who/whom choices tend to stick out as the obvious pair to choose from; and "why" is a very weak distractor.

But even with this help, how can the inexperienced teacher write distractors that sound right? One way is to look at the errors that students make on exercises or cloze passages. These errors can be used as distractors. Another source of distractors is errors on compositions. Consider these:

> When I was in Middle School 4 year ago I study english and didn't like ____. But since one year I know Canada familie, ____ have many opportunity for to practice my english. Which I like it now.

Because we are discussing grammar tests, we will not discuss the errors in mechanics (spelling, capitalization, and punctuation) in this student essay. One of several grammar items that we can see is the tense error, which is circled. "I **study** English" should be "I **studied** English." Prepare a question like the one below, if you have studied the past tense.

(3.4) Several years ago I ____ English.
★A. studied B. study C. have studied D. will study

If you have studied time words, you can use the error "**since** one year," which is also circled:

(3.5) I lived with them ____ one year.
A. since ★B. for C. during D. while

And if you have taught relative clauses, you can use the error "which I like it now," which is circled in the essay:

(3.6) English is a class which I like ____ now.
A. that B. it C. one ★D. ——

(Notice that choice "D" means that no word should be added.)

So far, we have been looking for distractors that sound right. But there are other things to keep in mind also. It is good not to confuse or tire your students by having them reread unnecessary material. Take out any repeated words from the distractors and put these in the stem.

(3.7) **(poor)** If I had a new fur coat, ____
A. I showed it to everyone. ★B. I'd show it to everyone. C. I've shown it to everyone. D. I'll show it to everyone.
(better) If I had a new fur coat, ____ it to everyone.
A. I showed ★B. I'd show C. I've shown D. I'll show

Also, it is best not to mix categories like the following:

(3.8) **(poor)** They just bought ____ furniture.

A. a few B. several ★C. some D. with
(better) They just bought ____
A. a few furnitures. B. several furnitures.
★C. some furniture. D. a furniture.

Item 3.8 above requires recognition of **furniture** as a noncount noun and recognition of the right determiner to use with this word. Choice "D" (with) is unsatisfactory because it is a preposition and not a determiner.

Alternate Forms of Multiple-Choice Completion

1. Space saver. The next example simply puts distractors inside the stem:

(3.9) Tom lives (A. at, ★B. on, C. in, D.——) Center Street.

2. Dialog context.

(3.10) "Did she ask you to go with her?"
"No, she asked someone ____ instead."
★A. else B. another C. other D. ——

3. Error identification. Unlike previous test items in this section, *error identification* does *not* require students to complete a sentence. Instead, they have to find the part containing an error. This kind of test question is particularly useful in testing grammar points for which there are few logical options, such as the choice between **few** and **a few, little** and **a little, some** and **any, much** and **many,** or **this** and **that.**

(3.11) One of the (A) girls lost her wallet and doesn't have (B) some (★C) money for (D) the game.

(or)

(3.12) I visited Netherlands/(★A) for a week last year/(B) while/(C) you were in school. (D) (no error) (E)

In addition to having students *identify* the error, it is also possible to have them give the correct form (**any** in 3.11 and **the Netherlands** in 3.12).

Advantages of Multiple-Choice Completion

1. It is impossible for students to avoid the grammar point being evaluated.
2. Scoring is easy and reliable.
3. This is a sensitive measure of achievement (and like other multiple-choice language tests, it allows teachers to diagnose specific problems of students).

Limitations of Multiple-Choice Completion

1. Preparing good items is not easy.
2. It is easy for students to cheat. (It is possible to create a second form of the test by rearranging the items, but this is time consuming for the teacher.)
3. It doesn't *appear* to measure students' ability to reproduce language structures (although in actual fact this kind of test *is* a good measure of the grammar subskill).
4. This can have a negative influence on classwork if used exclusively. (Students may see no need to practice writing if tests are objective.)

SIMPLE COMPLETION (SENTENCES)

Simple-completion items used for testing grammar consist of a sentence from which a grammatical element has been removed. An elementary item would be "He went __to__ school." An advanced open-ended item would be "I would have gone if __he had invited me__." Students may be asked to decide from the context what word or phrase to write in the blank; or they may be asked to write in an option from a list, or to change the form of a key word (such as **write** to **wrote**).

There are three steps to follow in preparing simple-completion grammar tests: (1) Select the grammar points that need to be tested; (2) provide an appropriate context; and (3) write good instructions. But it is also necessary to decide what kind of simple-completion question to use. Some are easier than multiple-choice completion, and some are much more difficult. Most of this section will deal with the three basic kinds of simple-completion grammar tests: (1) the option form, (2) the inflection form, and (3) the free-response form.

These three forms vary not only in difficulty but also in objectivity and in the degree of active or passive response that is required. As a result, you can tailor the test to the students that you have.

Your advance planning will determine which general question type to use. If you need to check mastery of many structures, you will probably select multiple-choice completion. If you have to test sentence combining, word order, or sentence transformation skill, you can use a *guided writing* procedure.

(3.13) Combine these two sentences:
She knew something. / He loved her.
(Answer) She knew that he loved her.

But if you want a quick way to check the mastery of a few specific points for only one or two classes of students, simple completion is ideal.

(3.14) He ______ (sleep) well when he was a child.

The Option Form

The easiest simple-completion items are like multiple-choice questions with only two options.

Directions: Complete the following sentences with "do" or "make."

(3.15) 1. He <u>made</u> a lot of money last year.
(3.16) 2. I always <u>do</u> my best.

This option form can easily be adapted from exercises in your textbook. Sometimes a new pair of options is given for each sentence.

(3.17) The <u>lost</u> child was crying for her mother. (losing, lost)

(3.18) The magician performed some <u>astonishing</u> tricks. (astonishing, astonished)

Often there are three or four choices listed, and at times even more. For example, here is a nine-option completion item from an ESL text. Students choose the best question word from among the following: **who, whom, where, what, when, why, how many, how much, how.**

QUESTION	ANSWER
(3.19) <u>When</u> did the clock stop running?	At twelve o'clock.
(3.20) <u>Why</u> were you late?	We ran out of gas.[1]

The Inflection Form

Testing the mastery of inflections provides for a productive response. These vary from simple comparatives to verb tense questions:

(3.21) He's the <u>tallest</u> (tall) person in the class.

(3.22) They <u>were</u> (be) in Colorado last week.

When students have to write in their own answer like this, you have to be careful about context. For example, new teachers might think that if they write a sentence like "He ____ (sing) a song," only "is singing" will fit. If they're testing the progressive, they may be disappointed to find that several other answers are possible, such as sings, sang, has been singing, had been singing, will sing, etc. This problem can be solved by giving part of the verb or adding more context.

(3.23) He is <u>singing</u> (sing). *(or)* He <u>is</u> singing now. (Add one word.)

(3.24) "What's Tom doing now?" "Oh, he <u>is singing</u> (sing)."

Another technique is to use a separate blank for each word in the verb phrase:

(3.25) He____ ____ ____ (sleep) for nearly an hour.
(Answer) He's been sleeping. *(or)* He has been sleeping.

A few teachers become desperate. They use grammatical terminology such as "Rewrite the sentence using the present perfect continuous." We don't recommend this. It would be better to accept any correct answer or to use multiple-choice questions instead.

The Free-Response Form

Sometimes a few simple terms can be used, if everybody in the class knows what they mean. The free-response form illustrates how that common terminology can occasionally be used. Here are some sentences from an ESL text:

Example: Add a question tag to these sentences:
(3.26) Hamlet was indecisive, wasn't he ?
(3.27) Polonius knew a lot of aphorisms, didn't he ?[2]

It is good to use an example to make sure that no one is confused. Here are some illustrations from a widely used ESL text.

Directions: Write in the missing part of the two-word verb.
(3.28) *Example:* "What time did he get up this morning?"
Directions: Write in a two-word verb that has the same meaning as the key word.
(3.29) *Example:* "Jack got up (arose) later than usual."[3]

The final example illustrates free response with a minimum amount of contextual control. (Here the conditional is being tested.)

(3.30) "You would get better sooner if ______."

These take longer to correct than other completion types, and they also take more language skill to evaluate properly. Consider a few acceptable ways that students could complete example 3.30: "if **you dressed warmer,**" "if **you'd see a doctor,**" "if **Mother**

were here," "if **we had some medicine for you.**" Obviously, this last kind of simple-completion question requires the most real productivity of all. It also provides flexibility; and it is perhaps the most communicative.

Advantages of Simple Completion (Sentences)

1. These are generally easier to prepare than are multiple-choice items.
2. These give the appearance of measuring productive skills because some items permit flexibility and original expression.
3. There is no exposure to incorrect grammatical forms.
4. These provide a sensitive measure of achievement.

Limitations of Simple Completion (Sentences)

1. These are usually more time consuming to correct than are multiple-choice questions. Not only can poor penmanship be a problem but also "irrelevant" errors beyond those being tested.
2. Occasionally students can unexpectedly avoid the structure being tested.

CLOZE PROCEDURE

Cloze tests are prose passages, usually a paragraph or more in length, from which words have been deleted. The student relies on the context in order to supply the missing words.

At the present time, no single test format is more popular than the cloze procedure. It is easy to prepare and rather easy to score. Teachers like it too because it is integrative–that is, it requires students to process the components of language simultaneously, much like what happens when people communicate. Moreover, studies have shown that it relates well to various language measures–from listening comprehension to overall performance on a battery of language tests. In brief, it is a good measure of overall proficiency.

But as we have seen in the introductory chapter, *proficiency* tests such as the cloze do have some limitations. For one thing, they usually don't measure short-term gains very well. A good *achievement* test could show big improvement on question tags studied over a two- to three-week period. But a proficiency test generally would not show much if any improvement. Fortunately a simple change in the cloze format can overcome this problem. After looking at regular cloze tests, we will discuss the modified cloze, which can evaluate grammar skills.

Before examining how to prepare this kind of test, let's consider briefly the principle that underlies it. The cloze is simply a story or essay from which a number of words have been deleted. We fill in the missing words much as we do while conversing. In a noisy restaurant, we guess at the words that we don't hear by relying on the whole conversation. So in cloze tests, the overall meaning and surrounding grammar help us replace the missing parts. Sentence-completion vocabulary and grammar items are similar in a way to cloze tests. Cloze passages simply have much larger contexts.

Preparing a Cloze Test

The steps in preparing a cloze test are simple: (1) Select an appropriate passage (e.g., from the reading material in your ESL class); (2) decide on the ratio of words to take out; (3) write the instructions and prepare an example. Each of these steps will be explained in the paragraphs that follow.

The first and most important step is to choose a story or essay on the right level. If your class uses an ESL reader, choosing a passage that is rather difficult for your students will simply frustrate them. So choose a passage that they can read with little or no difficulty. You can even use something that has already been read and discussed in class. They will not be able to answer the test from memory. The length of the selection depends on the number of blanks you plan to have. But most are not longer than 300 to 400 words. This means that you will often have to use only part of an article or story. When you do this, be sure your excerpt makes sense by itself. You might have to compose a sentence or two of your own to introduce or end your selection. (See the dictation discussion in Chapter 6.)

Also there are a few things to avoid: Usually we ignore a

passage that is full of proper nouns, numbers, and technical words. When these are left out, it is often impossible to know what to write in. Also, we usually do not pick an article containing a lot of quoted material. The latter might not be at the same level as the rest of the passage. But if there are only a few trouble spots in a good selection, you can edit or rewrite them.

With the passage chosen, you are ready to decide which words to take out. Leaving the first sentence or two and the last one as they are will help students understand the overall meaning. Words are then taken out at regular intervals—the shortest interval being one in five (every fifth word deleted) and the longest one in ten. The most frequently used deletion is one in seven. Unless the passage is quite easy, the one-in-five deletion may not give enough context and the one-in-ten can be somewhat inefficient. The following example shows that deleting every fifth word can make the passage too difficult for your students.

(3.31) **(poor)** (*Not enough context* for this passage) "We lost two superstars in 1977. Neither man's admirers have ____ able to understand the ____ of the other one. ____ this tells us something ____ the difference between the ____ that the two singers ____."[4]
(This is from a low-intermediate ESL reader. The missing words: been, success, And, of, generations, represent.)

How many words need to be deleted altogether? If you use the test by itself, we suggest about 50 blanks. This will require a passage of just over 350 words. Better still would be two different kinds of selections, with close to 200 words in each. But if your cloze is part of a larger test, you may get by with 25 to 30 blanks. Naturally, more blanks make the test increasingly stable and reliable.

An alternate form of this test is called "selected-deletion" cloze. Approximately the same percentage of words is removed. But now you can choose which words you want to leave out—such as only the content words or only the function words. Another application is to take out every seventh word *except* for duplications and proper nouns or numbers; when you find these, you can skip to the next word.

In taking a cloze test, students can normally do better if they look over the whole passage first. Therefore, it is good to prepare instructions that mention this. Here is a set of directions for students who have done cloze exercises in class:

> *Instructions:* First, read over the whole story quickly. Then read it carefully and fill in the blanks. Finally read it again to see that your words make sense.

And here is a sample set for those who have not had practice with cloze:

> *Instructions:* Here is a small story. Fifty words have been taken out of it. You must decide what goes in each blank. (1) Before you write anything, read the story quickly. (2) Then read it carefully and write a word in each blank. The word must fit the sentence. Write only *one* word in each blank. (3) When you finish, read over the story again and see if all of your words fit.

Scoring the Cloze

There are two possible ways to score cloze tests. One is to give credit for only the exact word from the story. Another is to allow full credit for equivalent words as well. Both methods rank students about the same, but students feel strongly that the second method is more "fair." We recommend allowing full credit for equivalent words (but *no* partial credit for words that are a little "off"). We do *not* recommend that non-native speakers decide what equivalent words to use. If the test is very important, you can give the cloze to a group of native speakers. Any word that *two* or more of these native speakers put in any blank you can count as a good equivalent. But suppose you aren't able to get people whose first language is English and you are a non-native speaker of English. Then use the exact-word scoring method, or ask a native English teacher to say which words are equivalents.

There are a few special problems that come up when scoring cloze. One of these is misspellings. Some teachers take off half a point for each different kind of spelling error. Many of us take off points for spelling only when it seems the required word is no longer recognizable. Then the student gets no credit for that answer. Another problem is bad handwriting. Here the same standard applies: no credit for words that the teacher cannot recognize. A third difficulty occurs when students use two or more words in the blank and the two words fit perfectly. Still no credit is given. Directions say that only one word is possible in each blank.

Adapting the Cloze to Test Grammar

It was mentioned earlier that regular cloze passages measure general ability in English, but certain kinds of selected-deletion cloze referred to above can measure grammar. One way is simply to delete prepositions, or you could delete some other grammar item that has been studied. For a measure of general grammatical ability, take out function words (pronouns, articles and determiners, auxiliary verbs, prepositions, and conjunctions). Here is a short passage from an ESL text that illustrates this procedure:

(3.32) Every day thousands of people jog. Why has jogging—running slowly for long distances—become so popular? Donald Robbins, who is forty-two years old ____(1) works in an office, began jogging ____(2) few years ago because he felt ____(3) was too fat. At first he ____(4) only run about 100 yards, and ____(5) took him almost three months to ____(6) able to run a full mile. ____(7) two years later, he ran in ____(8) eastern marathon race—over twenty-six miles.

____(9) you jog too? If you decide ____(10), be sure to ask your doctor ____(11) advice.

Does jogging cost much? No, ____(12) costs almost nothing. But most agree ____(13) good running shoes are very important. ____(14) protect your feet and legs from ____(15) shock of running on hard surfaces.

> If you start jogging, it could make your heart stronger and also help you to feel better about yourself. (*Key:* (1) and, (2) a, (3) he, (4) could, (5) it (anticipatory pronoun), (6) be, (7) But, (8) an, (9) Should, (10) to, (11) for, (12) it (personal pronoun), (13) that, (14) They, (15) the.)[5]

In preparing a selected-deletion grammar cloze like the one illustrated above, remember that it is not necessary to have exactly the same number of words between each blank. Be careful not to delete the same word too many times.

Alternate Forms of Cloze

There are many variations of the standard cloze. These do not have a fixed ratio of word deletions from a prose passage. Here are three that are referred to in this book:

1. Multiple-choice cloze. (See Chapter 2, p. 23.)
2. Selected-deletion cloze. (See discussion directly above "Adapting the Cloze to Test Grammar.")
3. Inflectional cloze. (See Chapter 2, p. 30.)

Advantages of Cloze

1. It is easy to prepare and quite easy to score.
2. It is a good measure of integrative English skills.
3. Standard cloze is a good measure of overall ability in English.

Limitations of Cloze

1. It is not a sensitive measure of short-term gains.
2. It is difficult for teachers who are non-native English speakers to choose acceptable equivalent words.

·ACTIVITIES·

A. LIMITED RESPONSE. (See pages 34 to 38.)

1. Write out five items to test students individually. If possible, use grammar points from your students' text.

a. Three commands should test prepositions of place (such as in, on, under, next to, between).

b. Two items should test understanding of either/or questions (such as "Am I sitting or standing?").

2. Choose two grammar points (preferably ones your students have studied). To test these grammar points, have students draw pictures on a sheet of paper. Write out instructions and indicate what grammar points you are testing.

3. Test the past tense with an action picture and a clock face. Provide the picture, the question, and the expected answer. (*Example:* Tell what she did this morning.
She wrote a letter [at 9:00].)

4. Test the use of **before** or **after** as a subordinator. (Or you may choose another subordinator—one your students have studied.) Find or sketch a set of two or three pictures that show a sequence of activities. Then write out instructions that tell your students what to do. Include the sketches, instructions, and appropriate sample student answer (*Example:* "Before he ate, he washed his car").

B. MULTIPLE-CHOICE COMPLETION. (See pages 38 to 43.)
1. Each of the following items has some defect. Indicate what the difficulty is, and then correct it by rewriting the question.

a. "Eva nearly won that race." / "Yes, ____ "
A. she ran well, did she?" B. she ran well, wasn't she?" C. she ran well, was she?" ⋆D. she ran well, didn't she?"

b. While she ____ the house, her children were playing outside.
A. has been cleaning ⋆B. cleaned C. has cleaned D. was cleaning

c. He has lived in this town for only a week and he already has ____ friends.
A. few ⋆B. a few C. not many D. your

d. "Mr. Adams, ____ I be excused from class tomorrow?"
A. ought to B. can ⋆C. may D. wouldn't

2. Construct a multiple-choice completion question for each of the following grammar points. Or choose five grammar points that you have taught to your students. Give the instructions and the answers.

a. The subordinator **although** (as in "Although he was tired, he walked to work").
b. Subject-verb agreement with some form of the verb **be** (as in "One of the boys was here last night").

c. **Since** as an expression of time (as in "They've been here since 10:00").

d. A question tag (as in "She works hard, doesn't she?").

C. SIMPLE COMPLETION (SENTENCES). (See pages 43 to 47.)

1. Write down as many words as you can (not phrases) that appropriately complete this sentence: "He walked . . . the house."

2. Prepare four two-option form items testing the too/enough contrast (that is, "too big to" versus "big enough to"). Prepare good contexts. Include the answers.

3. Prepare four verb-inflection items–a different verb and verb tense for each item. Include the *un*inflected form. Supply the answers. (*Example:* She ____ [drink] it this morning.)

4. Write four free-response items (see item 3.30). Each one should test a different grammar point. (One of these can be the conditional as in the example.) Name the grammar points being tested. Include two sample correct answers for each of the four items.

D. CLOZE PROCEDURE. (See pages 47 to 52.)

1. Write out the major problem that you see in the following cloze test. Disregard its short length.

> There was much conflict in early Vermont. It remained an unbroken wilderness until ____, when a French officer established Fort ____ on Isle La Motte. In 1924 Massachusetts ____ fearing attacks by the French and ____, built Fort Dummer near the present ____ of Brattleboro. The French forts at ____ and Crown Point were used as ____ for attacks. (*Key:* 1666, St. Anne, colonists, Indians, site, Chimney Point, bases)[6]

2. Two different cloze passages were prepared from a single essay. The actual key to each test is listed here, though the essay is not printed. Compare their usefulness as *grammar* tests. Key #1: basically, drawings, called, reappear, story, a, a, a, of, outlined, page, of. Key #2: by, can, the, in, to, so, Their, of, who, a, the, have.

3. Prepare a full-length cloze test. It should test grammar, and it should be on the right level for your students. Write out the instructions and the passage (with numbered blanks). Include a key at the end. *Optional activity:* Administer the test and choose equivalent correct answers. Tell what they are and how you chose them.

ANSWER KEY

B1

a. repeated words; b. two correct answers; c. mixed grammar points; d. divided usage

D1

too many proper nouns

D2

Excerpt 2 is better for testing grammar; function words have been deleted.

·CHAPTER FOUR·

PRONUNCIATION TESTS

This chapter on pronunciation tests presents a variety of ways to evaluate students' production and identification of the sounds, stress patterns, and intonation of English. After looking at ways to test beginning students in the limited-response section, you are introduced to multiple-choice hearing identification (evaluating how well students can recognize the differences in meaning that a sentence can have, depending on how the teacher pronounces various parts of it). The chapter concludes with a reading-aloud section that shows how to test a student's pronunciation by having him read something orally.

Tests devoted exclusively to pronunciation are rare today—much less common than tests of vocabulary and grammar. While a pronunciation exam could appropriately be used in a phonetics class, most ESL classes would include a few pronunciation items only when testing listening or speaking. Checking the individual sounds that students could pronounce was common during the audio-lingual period following World War II, but now there is a greater emphasis on broad listening and speaking goals. Many feel that too much stress used to be placed on pronunciation. One reason for this view is that even after much training, very few adolescents or adults ever achieve perfect pronunciation in their second language. Moreover, very effective communication is possible without complete mastery of this subskill.

All this does not mean that pronunciation is unimportant; it simply means that this language component is normally evaluated in conjunction with listening and speaking. Moreover, today's pronunciation items tend to incorporate context and *meaning.* On a speaking test, pronunciation becomes important when it interferes with communication. In brief, such test items can be useful, but they will not be the most frequently used in most ESL courses. While pronunciation items by themselves are not very effective in measuring real communication, they can at least measure progress made on specific points of pronunciation. Deciding what to test depends in part on how advanced your students are, in part on how accurate you think they should be, and in part on what you have been teaching. With beginning students, it makes sense to decide on what is most important in getting meaning across. For many teachers, this means evaluating students' recognition and production of intonation ("Did he go home?"↗"Yes, he did."↘)

Many teachers would also test stress, since faulty stress interferes with communication. For example, if a student says, "She wants the blue pén, not the red óne," it sounds for a moment that the choice is between a **pen** and something else such as a pencil. If the choice is actually between pens of two different colors, then we would expect a different stress pattern: "She wants the blúe pen, not the réd one."

Another matter often checked with beginning to intermediate students is vowel reduction, since so many words in English are affected. For instance, the vowel in the word "to" sounds like /uw/ when, for example, the word appears at the end of a sentence ("Who did he send the letter *to*?"), but in its normal position in a phrase ("going *to* town") its vowel "reduces" to /ə/ (or "schwa").

More advanced students can be evaluated in less critical areas such as in their ability to handle assimilation. Assimilation is where certain combinations of sounds (like /t/ and /y/ are pronounced as one sound ("can't you" becoming /kænčuw/).

But it is not productive to spend time evaluating small points that even native speakers pay little attention to. For example, some teachers spend time checking recognition of "juncture" (word or phrase boundaries) with contrasts like "I scream" and "ice cream." Such differences are hard to hear; and so-called "errors" almost never result in a lack of communication. Also it is not necessary to test linguistic matters such as phonetic symbols (/æ/, /iy/, /ǰ/, /ŋ/) or terminology (palatal assimilation, fricatives, diphthongs); knowledge of this information does not necessarily mean that students can pronounce English properly.

LIMITED RESPONSE

Individual Testing: Oral Repetition

Oral-repetition items are useful for students who cannot read or write English, because they can simply listen to what their teacher says to them and then repeat it. Yet oral repetition also has an advantage for those who are literate: Reading skills are not mixed with pronunciation skills. But oral repetition does have one major limitation: Some beginning students can mimic or imitate quite well, but they might not have developed much skill yet in pronouncing and using English. Therefore, results of an oral-repetition test could indicate *potential* for learning English as much as *present skill* in using the language.

Oral repetition is one of the easiest of all exams to prepare. No distractors are needed; no clever sentence frames are required, and no drawings need to be prepared. Furthermore, every pronunciation feature can be tested. In fact, in one short sentence, such as "Did you say I stole the meat?" we can evaluate the pronunciation of key vowels and diphthongs (/i/, /iy/, /uw/, /ey/, /ow/), important consonants such as the troublesome "th" (or /ð/), vowel reduction (the schwa in "the" and possibly in "you," which reduces quite often to /yə/ in rapid speech), word linking (sayI), assimilation in the "did" + "you" combination (/diǰə/), consonant clusters (/st/ in "stole"), pitch (notably on "stole" and "meat"), terminal intonation (↗), and timed stress or sentence rhythm.

As we can see, a single sentence can provide a wealth of test items, yet in preparing the test, we have to keep in mind the problem of scoring it. Inexperienced teachers pack too much into each item and the result is confusion and inaccuracy.

Recording the response on tape reduces the problem somewhat, but it is time consuming and boring to play the tape back again and again for the information that you need. A better way is not to test for many things at one time. For example, you could check final intonation on questions, including echo cues and question tags. These you can mix so that answers won't be given mechanically:

- Where did she put the broom?↘
- Is that it near the door?↗
- She didn't put it back in the closet?↗
- He cleaned the place up quite well, didn't he?↘

It's a good idea to have a separate sentence for each point you're testing, although this is not a firm rule. Many teachers are comfortable checking two things in one sentence. For example, it would be possible to listen for main stress and rising intonation in the same sentence: "Did it come yésterday?"↗

In preparing material to read aloud to your students, you can use exercises, dialogs, and readings from your ESL books; or you can make up your own. Some teachers prefer using part of an essay or story. This provides continuity from sentence to sentence, but it is often inefficient: You may have to read a lot to get the specific sounds or intonation you are interested in. This is why many teachers use unrelated sentences or construct their own story.

When reading the material aloud, do so at normal or near normal speed; and be sure to keep normal sentence rhythm. This of course includes joining the words in your phrases and keeping function words unstressed: "one of the pans" (/wənəvðəpænz/). Also, it is a good idea to say the sentence only once. In scoring this kind of test, listen only for the items marked on the key ("He said he <u>could</u> come."). Ignore other errors.

Give instructions orally, and keep them simple. For example, you might say, "I will read some sentences to you. Listen carefully. I will read each one only once. After each one, I will stop; then you say it back to me."

Group Testing: Hearing Identification

Strictly speaking, the ability to hear and identify various sounds (auditory perception) is a listening skill, but good pronunciation depends on how well we hear what is spoken. Therefore, we include items of "hearing identification" as one kind of pronunciation test. These can be simple enough for little children and adult beginners.

For beginners, the use of visuals in testing can emphasize the difference in meaning between words which sound similar. In this way, testing can reinforce teaching. For example, here is a set of three pictures. The student listens to a sentence in which "the" makes a big difference. He must be able to identify the word "the" (even though it is unstressed and its vowel reduced): "The box is in the back of the truck." Those who hear the second "the" will know that the third frame (C) is correct.

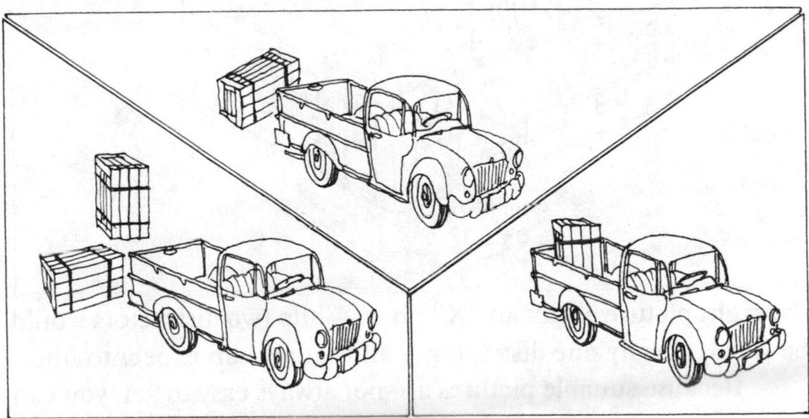

The illustration above captures a distinction that hinges upon the presence or absence of a consonant sound. But a difference in meaning can be signaled as well by word stress, and this can also be tested with pictures. For example, simple line drawings can contrast "He has a toy stóre" with "He has a tóy store." The first sentence refers to a child's toy that is made to look like a store. The second sentence refers to a store where toys are sold. The illustration we have used requires no speaking or writing on the part of the student. He can draw a circle around

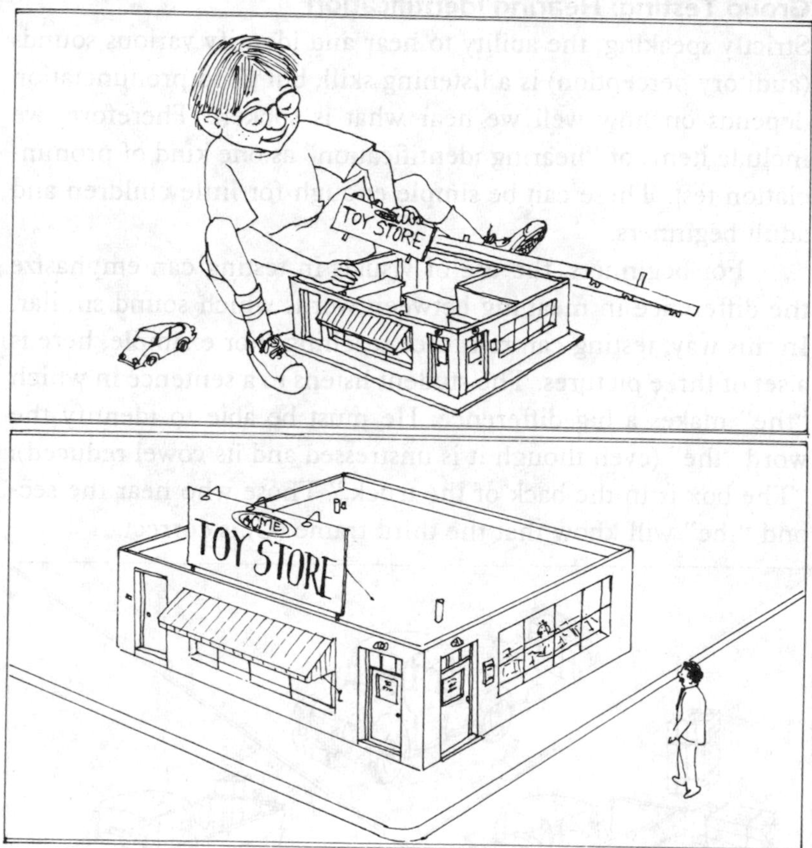

the right picture or put an "X" on it. While two distractors would be ideal, usually one distractor is all that we can expect to find.

Because suitable pictures are not always easy to get, you can use pairs of sentences instead. Students listen to two short sentences and decide if they are the same or different. Beginning students can circle "S" for "same" and "D" for "different." For example, if they heard, "What a big mouse," / "What a big mouth," the correct response would be "D". But we have to be careful when repeating sentences like this. Often our intonation changes quite unintentionally, and the student might circle "D" because of this difference in intonation.

It is possible of course to test intonation on purpose. Compare these two sentences (which would be presented orally and not in writing): "It's raining."↘ / "It's raining?"↗ Again the student would circle "D".

Alternate Forms of Limited-Response Items

1. Substitution drill. (The cue word can be spoken or written for your students.)

- Grapes aren't cheap now. (figs) /gz/
- He doesn't have to leave yet. (his brother) /ð/

2. Phrase items.

- into the house /ə/
- wrote a note /′˘′/

3. Sentence completion. (This can be cued with pictures.)

- Pencils use lead, but pens use . . . . /ŋ/ [ink]
- The American flag is red, . . . , and blue. /hw, w/ [white]

Advantages of Limited-Response Items

1. *(Oral repetition)* These are very easy to prepare.
2. *(Oral repetition)* These enable us to test students who can't read yet. Also they do not mix reading comprehension and pronunciation.
3. *(Oral repetition)* These can test virtually all pronunciation features.
4. *(Hearing identification)* These combine pronunciation and meaning.
5. *(Hearing identification)* These enable us to test students with rather limited language skills.

Limitations of Limited-Response Items

1. *(Oral repetition)* These possibly test aptitude to learn English as much as present skill in pronouncing English.
2. *(Oral repetition)* These are time consuming when administered individually. They can be administered in a language lab, but the teacher must still listen to tapes individually.
3. *(Oral repetition)* There is a need for a native speaker to model the sentence.
4. *(Hearing identification)* It is often difficult to think of suitable sketches or find suitable pictures.
5. *(Hearing identification)* There is a somewhat limited number of testing options. For example, consider the difficulty of representing contextualized contrasts of ramble-rumble, weird-geared, cud-could.

MULTIPLE-CHOICE HEARING IDENTIFICATION

Hearing-identification items can of course be used with students who are literate in their second language as well as with those who are not yet literate. In addition, students who can read some English may be evaluated by using multiple-choice hearing-identification items. These may be in either paraphrase or appropriate-response form.

Until fairly recently, sound contrasts such as those in **cap** and **cab** were often tested in isolation with little or no concern for meaning. Now we generally contextualize such words so that sound contrasts are associated with differences in meaning. For instance, we might say to our students, "He bought a new cab." They would need to understand whether we had said **cat** or **cap** or **cab.** To emphasize the difference in meaning of these three choices, we would have them choose the best paraphrase or synonym of what they heard.

(4.1) *(students hear)*
"He bought a new cab."
(students read)
A. animal B. hat *C. car

Another way to contextualize vowel and consonant contrasts is to use appropriate-response options. In the following item, we check student ability to differentiate among "I feel," "I fell," and "I'll feel":

(4.2) *(students hear)*
"I feel sick."
(students read)
A. Did you? *B. Do you? C. Will you?

The meaning behind intonation contrasts (like "He's her brother."↘ and "He's her brother?"↗) can also be evaluated by using appropriate-response items:

(4.3) *(students hear)*
"He's her brother."

(students read)

★A. Oh, I didn't know that. B. Yes, I thought you knew that. C. Why do you ask?

Contrasting either/or intonations can be evaluated the same way. Notice the responses appropriate to each question:

(4.4) "Would you like soup or salad?" ("Yes, thank you . . .")

(4.5) "Would you like soup or salad?" ("Some salad, please.")

A good way to evaluate contrastive stress is by using multiple-choice paraphrase. As we know, a sentence such as "Jack just walked into the store" can express different meanings, depending on which word is stressed. A heavy stress on "store" could mean that the boy went into the **store** and not into the **school;** a heavy stress on "Jack" could mean that it was **Jack** and not **Mary** who went into the building. Our item, therefore, could take this form:

(4.6) *(students hear)*

"Jack just walked ínto the store."

(students read)

A. It wasn't Mary. B. He didn't run. ★C. He didn't walk out of it.

An Alternate Form of Multiple-Choice Hearing Identification

Sentence completion. (Here, checking the **hid / hit / 'll hit** contrast.)

(4.7) *(students hear)*

"She hit the thief . . ."

(students read)

★A. in the face. B. from the police. C. tomorrow.

Advantage of Multiple-Choice Hearing Identification

This is a helpful combination of pronunciation and meaning.

Limitation of Multiple-Choice Hearing Identification

It is difficult to prepare suitable distractors. (Teachers whose own English is somewhat limited will probably want to use a different technique than this to test pronunciation.)

READING ALOUD

One of the most common ways of checking pronunciation is to have students read something aloud. Like oral repetition, it provides excellent control. One problem, however, is that the skill of reading aloud is different from that of talking conversationally. In fact, many native speakers of English don't read English aloud very well: Sometimes they give spelling pronunciations, and because they see individual words on the page, they tend to say them separately rather than linking them as they do in normal speech. Despite this limitation, reading aloud is a rather popular way to test the pronunciation of students who can *read* English. Naturally it is an ideal way to test mastery of sound-symbol correspondence (for example, "said" = /sɛd/, not /sayd/).

There are three points to keep in mind when preparing reading-aloud items: (1) When using lists of sentences, evaluate only one or two points per sentence; (2) use natural language; and (3) avoid signaling to the student which pronunciation point you are testing. Let's look at these three points in more detail.

1. Evaluate only one or two items per sentence. As in oral-repetition items, much could be tested in a single sentence. The problem comes in trying to evaluate a number of pronunciation points simultaneously; it is extremely difficult to be accurate and consistent when checking a number of things at the same time. Student progress in mastering specific sounds, stress, and intonation can be tested more reliably if only one or two features are looked at per sentence. For example, this sentence looks at the contrast between the voiced "th" pronunciation and the "d" pronunciation:

(4.8) My fa<u>th</u>er feels quite ba<u>d</u> about it. (The student's copy would not be underlined.)

And this sentence checks the use of rising intonation:

(4.9) Do you need any help? ↗ (The student's copy would not have the intonation cue.)

2. Use natural language. While tongue twisters and rhymes may occasionally be used in class, our tests should reflect the ability to communicate in more natural everyday language. Items 4.8 and 4.9 above illustrate natural language, but the two that follow use unlikely, strange language to test juncture contrasts (4.10) and the /br/ consonant cluster (4.11).

(4.10) **(poor)** I scream for ice cream.
(4.11) **(poor)** I bought the bread that his brother brings.

3. Avoid signaling the point being tested. Often a student can produce a sound correctly if he concentrates on it, but in normal speech he may not do so well. In order, then, to get an accurate measure of how students normally express themselves in English, it is best *not* to let them know the specific pronunciation point being tested in each sentence. Items like 4.11 above, unwittingly signal exactly what it is that is being evaluated. Some teachers love to use minimal pairs on tests (words that are pronounced exactly alike except for one slight difference in sound). But sentences using minimal pairs often sound unnatural, and they usually alert the student to what is being tested. For example, sentences 4.12 and 4.13 both test the voiced "th" and the "v" sounds, but in 4.12 the minimal pair (leather / lever) shows the student what we're looking for.

(4.12) **(poor)** The leather is near the lever.
(4.13) **(better)** She loves her brother.

Keep in mind also that it is not necessary to illustrate pairs of similar but contrasting sounds in the same sentence; for example, "brother" in 4.13, which includes a voiced "th," might appear in one sentence and "loves" in another. Finally, it should be pointed out that there is no need to eliminate minimal pairs completely from phonology tests: Sample test item 4.14 shows how a minimal pair can be properly used to test contrastive stress. (There would be no stress marks on the student paper.)

(4.14) They want you to saíl the boat, not séll it.

For teachers with special training in phonology and access to a tape recorder, carefully prepared *paragraphs* can be provided for students to read aloud. These are able to provide natural language in a much broader context than is found in sentence items. If the teacher is willing to replay the tape several times, he can check for a variety of matters such as thought groups, stress, rhythm, and intonation as well as vowels and consonants. The main problem, however, is deciding how to score a passage where so many things are being evaluated. Because of this difficulty, most teachers are better off using separate sentences with a fixed number of points per item (like 4.8). The paragraph context, then, would normally be used for diagnostic purposes rather than for testing.

Example 4.15 is an excerpt from a commercial diagnostic selection. Unlike the individual sentences that checked only one or two pronunciation features at a time, this checks a large number of matters: vowels, consonants, intonation, stress, etc.

(4.15) (1) When a student from another country comes to study in the United States, he has to find the answers to many questions, and he has many problems to think about. (2) Where should he live? (3) Would it be better if he looked for a private room off campus or if he stayed in a dormitory? . . . [1]

In conclusion, our major concern is to select material that sounds natural; and we need to emphasize that passages be read aloud naturally. Test instructions should emphasize the need for naturalness: "In a few minutes you will read the following material aloud to your teacher. But first you should become familiar with it. Read it over silently now. Then when you read it aloud, do so smoothly and naturally."

Alternate Reading-Aloud Items: Paper and Pencil

1. Stress Marking. Students silently read each item and then simply circle the letter of the word or syllable that would be stressed when no special emphasis is required for a unique context. Success on this kind of test shows that a student knows the rules of stress, but it doesn't necessarily indicate that he *uses* proper stress.

A B C *D
(4.16) He's in the basement. (*no* special contrastive stress)

A B *C
(4.17) intervene (syllable stress)

2. Sound-symbol. (Again, students read the item silently and circle the right answer. There are rules for pronouncing various combinations of letters. This item checks knowledge of the "o" in "short position.")

(4.18) (Which vowel sound is different?)

A	*B	C	D
go	got	close	smoke

Advantages of Reading-Aloud Items

1. They are easy to prepare.
2. They provide good control.
3. They test almost all pronunciation features.
4. They can test how to pronounce spelling combinations.

Limitations of Reading-Aloud Items

1. They are limited to those who can read.
2. There is not a direct relationship between ability to read aloud and pronunciation in normal conversation. Sentence rhythm is probably least accurately represented with this technique.

· ACTIVITIES ·

A. LIMITED RESPONSE. (See pages 59 to 63.)

1. Oral repetition: testing students individually. Choose four different pronunciation problems of your students and prepare a sentence illustrating each one—a sentence for your students to listen to and repeat. Or you can use the four pronunciation problems below:

a. Write out two sentences in which students must use the vowel sounds in "could" and "moon." (*Example:* "He should be here at noon.")

b. Write two sentences testing consonant clusters.

c. Write out two sentences testing syllable stress.

d. Write out two sentences testing rising intonation.

2. Hearing identification: testing students in groups.

a. Find (or sketch) one or two pictures that illustrate a pronunciation problem related to vowels or to consonants. Include the pictures. Make sure that you have at least one good distractor.

Example: "Please **sell** the boat."
(distractor = sail)

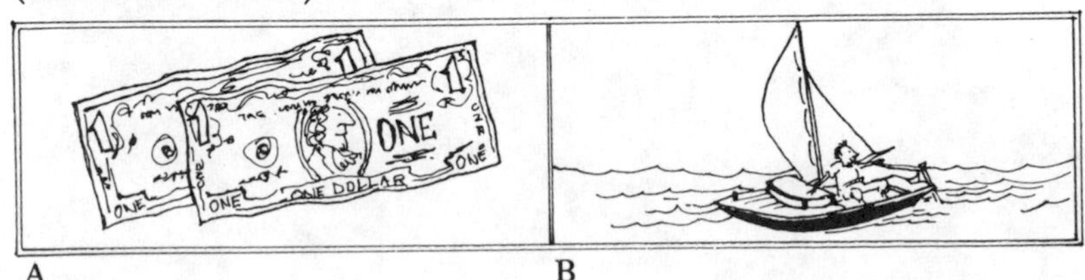

A B

b. Prepare a question on stress or intonation. Use sketches for your options. Write out your instructions and provide the answer.

Examples: (the first = stress; the second = intonation)
"He has a tóy store."

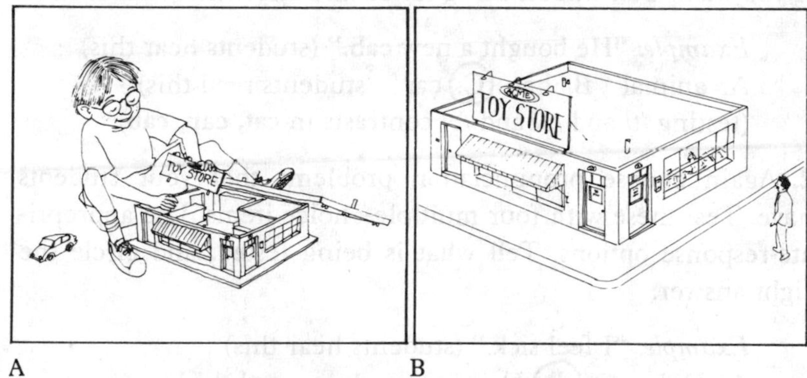

A B

"It's raining?" ↗

A B

c. Write out five "same-different" items. Test a different pair of vowels or consonants in each. Tell what is tested in each sentence.

B. MULTIPLE-CHOICE HEARING IDENTIFICATION. (See pages 64 to 66.)

1. Think of problems that your students have with vowels and consonants. Then prepare four sentences to test these problems. The example provides three choices, but since three good options are often difficult to find, you may use only two choices if you wish. Tell what is being tested and circle the right answer.

> *Example:* "He bought a new **cab.**" (students hear this)
> A. animal B. hat (C.) car (students read this)
> (testing /t/ and /p/ and /b/ contrasts in **cat, cap, cab**)

2. Again choose pronunciation problems that your students have. Test these with four multiple-choice items. Use appropriate-response options. Tell what is being tested, and circle the right answer.

> *Example:* "I feel sick." (students hear this)
> A. Did you? (B.) Do you? (students read this)
> (testing the /ɛ/ and /iy/ contrast in **fell** and **feel**)

C. READING ALOUD. (See pages 66 to 69.)

1. These are weak reading-aloud items. They "show" the student what is being tested. Tell what is tested in each sentence. Then make up better sentences. You do not have to use the same key words.

a. It would be wiser to clean the visor.
b. A myth is quite pithy, don't you think?
c. I wince at those runts in long pants.
d. He told me your street was quite straight.

2. These items require you to prepare sentences for students to read aloud. They should test the problems indicated.

> *Example:* "She's a wonderful singer, isn't she?" (They read this aloud.) Correct intonation = ↘. See item (a) below.
> a. Problem: Some students use only rising intonation on tag questions.

b. Problem: Some misplace the stress on words like "newspaper."

c. Problem: Some substitute a "t" sound for "th" in words like "both."

d. Problem: Some pronounce "lace" the same way that they do "less."

e. Problem: Some pronounce "asked" as though it were a two-syllable word.

ANSWER KEY

C1

a. (/w/ and /v/ contrast); b. (/θ/ and /I/); c. (/ts/ consonant cluster); d. (/str/ consonant cluster)

·PART II·

TESTING COMMUNICATION SKILLS

Part I of this book discussed the testing of language components. These components are only some of the "ingredients" in communication. It is important to realize that these ingredients do not represent communication skills per se, nor collectively do they add up to communication itself. Actual communication is more complex than that.

In Part II, we look at tests that measure actual communication in the real world. Even here though, some attention will be given to components, such as punctuation in the area of writing. Generally, however, we will be concerned with measuring integrative skills: These combine elements like vocabulary and grammar as well as matters beyond the sentence level, such as writer's purpose or even social appropriateness.

Chapter 5 presents various ways to test reading comprehension; Chapter 6 discusses approaches to the testing of writing; Chapter 7 shows basic ways to test listening comprehension; and Chapter 8 covers different options for testing speaking. Each chapter is divided into three or four sections, the first section presenting ways to evaluate beginning language learners. As in Part I, an Activities unit concludes each chapter. This is designed to help you develop skill in preparing various kinds of exam questions.

·CHAPTER FIVE·

READING TESTS

Tests of reading come in a wide variety of forms and evaluate a broad spectrum of reading activities. These range from pre-reading concerns (learning the Roman alphabet, for example, or word-attack skills) to reading comprehension, reading speed, and skimming techniques. Advanced and more specialized applications include translation, reading aloud, and reading literature. Reading *speed* is especially important for students with lots of out-of-class reading to do. Skimming is handy for people who need to hunt for information in print: This includes reading a newspaper as well as doing research in a library. The advanced applications are helpful for translators as well as radio and television announcers. Many students at the advanced level can use skills of literary analysis for school and leisure.

But the heart of reading evaluation in most schools is reading *comprehension,* and that will be our main emphasis in this chapter. After a brief look at limited-response techniques (notably in the area of pre-reading), we will discuss how to test sentence comprehension and passage comprehension.

LIMITED RESPONSE

For those teaching beginning reading, informal techniques of evaluation are recommended such as exercises and individual practice. Early testing is often limited to reading subskills, the most common being vocabulary (see Chapter 2). In addition, "word-attack" skills usually need attention on the beginning level. Here we see if the student can tell the difference fairly rapidly between various combinations of letters in English words.

The most typical test of this skill is the "same-different" technique, which is also used as a reading exercise in an occasional ESL text:

(5.1)	sad	sat	S (D)
(5.2.)	red	red	(S) D
(5.3)	meat	meet	S (D)

This can also be used with phrases:

Same-Different Phrases.

(5.4)	from the mayor / for the mayor	S (D)
(5.5)	with her brother / with her brother	(S) D

A similar testing arrangement has the student circle the odd item (notice that these are not necessarily minimal pairs).

(5.6)	net	net	(ten)
(5.7)	naps	(span)	naps

A third form uses a key word. Working rapidly, students have to circle the matching word from a list of four items.

(5.8) **pots:**

stop	pods	(pots)	spot

(5.9) **figure:**

(figure)	finger	fissure	ringer

Directions for this kind of test should be very simple. They can be read aloud by the teacher to help those whose reading is limited. If necessary, directions can even be given in the native language. Here are some sample instructions:

> "Each item has two words. In some items the words are the same. But in other items the words are different. When the two words are the *same,* draw a circle around 'S.' When the two words are *different,* draw a circle around 'D.' Work quickly. You have only ten minutes."

Example:

too	to	S (D)
in	in	(S) D

Besides limited-response vocabulary practice and these "same-different" techniques, there are simple sentence-level and even simple passage-comprehension items that can be used with students whose English is quite limited. These rather elementary sentence and passage questions will be discussed in the following two sections.

Alternate Forms of Limited-Response Items

1. Advanced odd items. The student still looks for the word that is different from the others. But now all three can be different, or all three can be the same. If only one word is different, he circles the odd word. If each word is different, he checks the "All Different" column. If all three are the same, he checks the "All the Same" column.

	Items			**All Different**	**All the Same**
(5.10)	speak	peaks	seeks	✓	
(5.11)	peace	peace	peace		✓
(5.12)	(into bed)	in the bed	in the bed		

2. Key word and odd option. There is only one difference between this alternate form and the original. Originally, we found the word that matched the key item. Now we find the word that does *not* match the key item, in short, the *different* word:

(5.13) **pleasure:** (pleasing) pleasure pleasure pleasure

(5.14) **want to go:** want to go want to go want to go (won't go)

Advantages of Limited-Response Items

1. These are quite easy to construct and score.

2. Only the recognition of letters is required, making this a simple task for beginning students.

Limitations of Limited-Response Items

1. This is not an integrative skill involving actual reading.
2. Overemphasis on this technique could reduce reading speed.

TESTING SENTENCE COMPREHENSION

There is no need to test comprehension of an essay if students still have difficulty understanding a sentence. Sentence comprehension must precede essay comprehension. Some sentence-level comprehension items are good for beginning students. Some elementary questions simply ask for the right picture to be circled. There are other questions that ask only for a one-word response. Besides their suitability for those students with limited skill in English, there is another good reason to use these types of questions: Much of what we read every day appears in only a single sentence or phrase—"Keep Off the Grass," "Open Other End," "No Trespassing," "Help Wanted."

We will begin this section with examples of sentence-comprehension questions that are designed for beginners. Then we will look at more challenging sentence-comprehension items, which can be used with more advanced students. These may ask for an appropriate paraphrase. In such questions, we check vocabulary, grammar, and sometimes even social appropriateness at the same time.

Elicitation Techniques

1. Picture Cues. We will start with questions that simply ask for the right picture to be circled. For the set of pictures on the next page, we can use the sentence:

(5.15) The children are playing on their new toy.

Students would pick the second picture. More obvious sentences can be prepared for students with less reading skill ("Mother is pushing the children on the tricycle"). From the larger picture we can prepare true-false items: for example,

(5.16) The robber cannot see the TV. T F

Or yes-no questions could be asked:

(5.17) Is the lady reading the newspaper? yes no

In example 5.15, we used multiple-choice *pictures.* It is of course possible to have multiple-choice questions on a single picture. For instance,

(5.18) The robber is successful because ___
A. he doesn't see the family. B. the family is at home in the living room. C. it is dark outside.
*D. the family doesn't hear him.

Here more reading is involved. This kind of question is usually more difficult than the true-false or yes-no item.

There are one or two problems that come up when using questions like these. Look at the following sentence: "The robber is oblivious of the family." Here everything might depend on one difficult word, "oblivious." Therefore, this item is really testing vocabulary.

2. Phrase and Sentence Cues. One of the simplest forms of sentence comprehension is the true-false sentence. It is used with beginners. The student looks for truths, untruths, or impossibilities:

(5.19) The sun sets in the east. T (F)
(5.20) She is my brother. T (F)

Teaching and testing the recognition of *signs* can be an interesting activity. What we test depends naturally on the age and interests of our students, and on what we teach. The following is a simple matching task. It asks only for the location of the sign. Students must understand the meaning of the location. Symbols can be used if necessary:

	Location	**Sign**
(5.21)	1. Park	A. Fasten Seat Belts
(5.22)	2. Restaurant	B. Beware of the Dog

(5.23) 3. Hotel	C. Please Do Not Walk on the Grass
(5.24) 4. Home	D. Dangerous Curve
(5.25) 5. Highway	E. Please Wait to be Seated by Hostess
(5.26) 6. Airplane	F. In Case of Fire, Do Not Use Elevators
(5.27) 7. Supermarket	G. No Smoking in Lavatories
	H. Self-Serve Pumps
	I. Express Checkout 8 Items or Less
	J. No Salesmen or Solicitors
	K. Sorry. No Checks or Credit Cards
	L. Check Out Time 1:00 p.m.
	M. No Shirt No Shoes No Service
	N. Shake Well Before Using

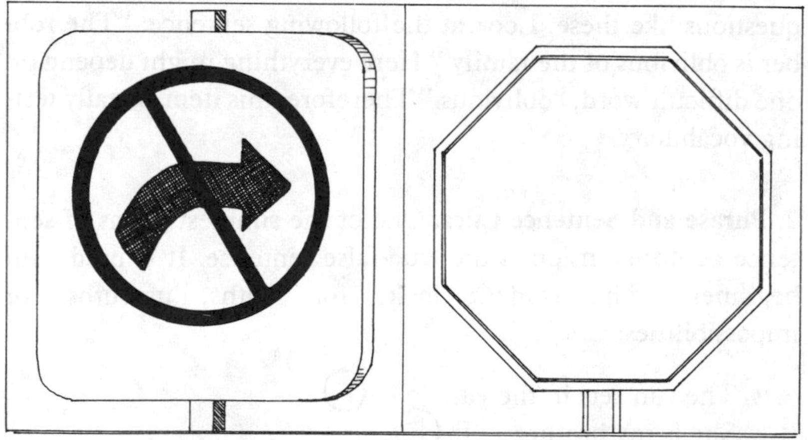

This can also be used as a pre-test. Some signs use technical low-frequency words ("No loitering," "High voltage," "Do not bend or staple"); understanding these requires students to become familiar with new vocabulary items. Other signs make frequent use of the imperative ("Open other end") and the negative ("Please do not litter"), for example; understanding these signs requires familiarity with the grammatical structures that are used.

The paraphrase is a good way to check for more exact or detailed comprehension of phrases and sentences.

(5.28) "Please Wait to Be Seated by the Hostess."
A. Sit near the hostess. ★B. The hostess will show you where to sit. C. There are no seats for you at this time.

The meaning of complex grammatical structures such as the conditional is often the key to the meaning of an entire passage. Paraphrase items like the one that follows check the meaning of such structures.

(5.29) "She can come if she wants to."
A. She wants to come. B. She will come. ★C. She has permission to come.

However, we see that items like 5.30 do not necessarily use a paraphrase of the entire sentence.

(5.30) "Although my friend Senator Ashmore is a man of great honesty and integrity, I find his well-written proposal totally unacceptable."
A. The speaker has found the bad proposal. B. The senator liked the honesty and integrity of his friend. ★C. The speaker doesn't like the Senator's proposal.

There are three cautions to keep in mind when preparing sentence and phrase items: (1) Don't make the answer rely on knowledge of facts that have nothing to do with language skill. For example, here is a poor true-false question that requires the student to know details of United States geography: "Cincinnati is west of Detroit." Students might understand what is being said but miss the item because they don't know the location of these two cities. (2) Unless you are testing cultural facts, don't make the answer depend on a knowledge of a specific culture. Here is another weak true-false item: "Easter is on Saturday." Students who are not Christians may not know that Easter is on Sunday. (3) When preparing multiple-choice items, make the choice simple and clear. In this poor question, the paraphrase options are expressed in language that is much more difficult to understand than the original statement.

(5.31) **(poor)** "No Shirt, No Shoes, No Service."
A. No articles of wearing apparel are available for purchase. *B. Unless one is properly attired, he will be refused service. C. One must remove certain articles of clothing for given situations.

Instruction Preparation

Where beginning students all speak the same language, instructions can be given in the native language, if necessary. When a set of pictures is used, you can prepare directions like the following:

> *Instructions:* First look at these pictures. Then read the sentence. It describes one of the pictures. Draw a circle around that picture.

Here are instructions for true-false statements:

> *Instructions:* Read these sentences. Some say strange things like "He **drank** his bicycle." (We **ride** a bicycle. We don't **drink** it.) Some are false like "Rain falls **up.**" (It falls **down,** not **up.**) For these sentences, circle "F" ("F" means "false"). For the other (good) sentences, circle "T" ("T" means "true").

For much more advanced students, these directions could be used with sentence-paraphrase items:

> *Instructions:* Three paraphrases follow each of the following sentences. The paraphrases may refer to just part of the sentence or to the entire sentence. Circle the letter of the *best* paraphrase.

Alternate Forms of Sentence Comprehension

We have already discussed some alternate forms of sentence comprehension—that is, we can test phrases as well as sentences.

We can use pictures with sentences or sentences alone. We can have the picture circled, or we can use true-false or yes-no questions with pictures.

In addition, we can use true-false questions without a picture. Here is a multiple-choice alternate form of this last question type:

(5.32) The sun rises in the ____
A. north. *B. east. C. south.

Advantages of Sentence-Comprehension Items

1. It is rather easy to write true-false items on pictures.
2. These are good for testing the skills of near beginning students.
3. This is a rapid way to test reading comprehension.

Limitations of Sentence-Comprehension Items

1. Finding good pictures can be rather time consuming.
2. Not all reading skills are covered in sentence-comprehension questions.

TESTING PASSAGE COMPREHENSION

So far in this chapter, we have looked at ways to test students whose reading skill is quite limited. We began with limited-response items that check students' ability to tell the difference between words that look very similar to each other. Then we saw how to check sentence comprehension through the use of pictures. We next observed how true-false responses could be used to indicate understanding of the basic idea expressed in a sentence. We also saw how common signs could be used in testing reading comprehension—by having students indicate the location of the sign or a paraphrase of it. And we learned that paraphrase can also be used to check the meaning of advanced grammatical structures which can influence the meaning of entire paragraphs.

We have finally arrived at the most integrative and challenging kind of reading test type—passage comprehension.

Context Selection

It is interesting nowadays to notice how many unusual "passages" or "contexts" that students are introduced to in an ESL class. Sometimes these unusual passages appear in modern ESL readers, and sometimes teachers—particularly teachers of secondary school students—collect practical reading items from the community for use in class. Besides the usual articles and stories, these may include advertisements, want ads, business and social letters, driver's license and loan applications, bank statements, rental and sales agreements, and mail order catalogs. Other reading materials may include texts from other classes at school such as biology, history, or chemistry. ESL reading instruction may also give attention to other school-related written material such as tables and graphs, blackboard summaries, duplicated handouts, notes, and notices.

Selecting what to test depends of course on what kind of reading matter you have used with your students. It is not necessary to restrict your test questions to the traditional essay if you have exposed students to a variety of written contexts. For example, look at these two rather unusual "passages" and the rather challenging comprehension questions that accompany them.

(5.33) 75 Gremlin. 6 cyl 2 dr 4 spd A-1 cond. 20 MPG city 8 trk AM/FM P.S. P.B., auto/cruise bucket seats Terms 379-1829 after 5.
This automobile has ____
A. an automatic transmission. B. a radio but no stereo. *C. cruise control. D. air conditioning.

(5.34) What is the best generalization we can make, based on the table on the next page?
*A. Increased production can lower the cost of a product. B. Goods were more expensive early in the century than later on. C. There is an increasing interest in mechanical inventions. D. People are less interested in items that cost more money.

DATA ON THE MODEL "T" FORD

YEAR	PRICE	NUMBER PRODUCED (in round numbers)
1909	$950	10,500
1910	$780	18,500
1911	$690	34,500
1912	$600	78,500
1913	$550	170,000[1]

The first passage requires some knowledge of cars and newspaper want ads; it is lexically oriented, and it requires an understanding of abbreviations used in newspaper advertisements: 75 = 1975; cyl = cylinders; dr = doors; spd = speed; cond = condition; MPG city = miles per gallon in the city; 8 trk = 8 track stereo; AM/FM = radio frequencies; P.S. and P.B. = power steering and power brakes; auto/cruise = automatic cruise control; after 5 = after 5:00 p.m.

The second passage requires students to be able to make inferences. They need to recognize that there is a probable relationship between the increased number of cars produced (see the column at the right) and the decrease in the cost per car (see middle column).

Question Techniques for Beginners

There are two useful approaches for testing beginning students who can read simple passages. One of these is true-false items, and the other is the matching technique. True-false items are rather easy to prepare, and for beginning students they are easier than regular multiple-choice items. Here is an example:

> Among the American Negroes in the southern states, work songs played an integral part in fashioning a folk music which was later to become jazz. These had been part of the West African's musical experience at home. And now they were transported to a new envi-

ronment. In America they were found to be of no little importance to the slaves' output of work.[2]

(5.35) Jazz is related to the work songs of American blacks. *T F

(5.36) Work songs were not helpful in getting more work done. T *F

One problem with true-false questions is that the student might simply guess the right answer. If concerned about this, you can make a correction for guessing: Just subtract the number wrong from the number right. This is their new score. (We can see why this is done, when we recall that on a true-false test, a student could get 50 percent of the answers right simply by guessing. In other words, if he knew 50 items on a 100-item test but guessed at the other 50, he might get a score of 75 [50 + 25 that he guessed right]. But if we subtract the number that he missed [25] from the number he got right [75], the result is 50–the number of items that he actually knew the answer to.

A "guessing correction" can also be made for regular multiple-choice tests. Normally we use a correction only when the test is timed, and many of the students do not have a chance to finish. This encourages guessing. The correction is made by dividing the number of items wrong by the number of distractors and subtracting this from the number of correct answers. For four-option items this is the number right minus the number wrong divided by 3, or $R - \frac{W}{3}$. For three-option items, this is $R - \frac{W}{2}$ [remember that of the *three* choices, *one* is the correct answer and *two* are distractors].)

A second useful approach for testing beginning students who can read simple passages is the matching technique. This procedure simply has students match material in the passage with material in the question. It is like "copy work" in beginning writing classes. For example, a question such as the following might be written on the "jazz" passage:

(5.37) "What played an integral part in fashioning folk music?"

★A. work songs B. jazz C. a new environment
D. Americans

Notice that the question and the answer are lifted right from the original passage. This gives some practice in handling questions, but little comprehension is required. A variation on this procedure asks students simple questions on dialogs that they have practiced in class.

(5.38) ANN: "Mr. Martin never works in the garage."
KEN: "Yes, he does. He worked in the garage last Saturday."
When was he working?
A. in the garage B. Mr. Martin ★C. last Saturday[3]

We can see that short test passages like this often concentrate on grammar or vocabulary.

Question Techniques for More Advanced Students

1. Standard Multiple-Choice. There are many ways to test reading. One of the best is a reading passage followed by multiple-choice questions. We have already mentioned the variety of sources available. Another is books from other classes; they can be used when all your students have the same classes in school. Naturally you can use readings from your own English course, but be careful to give everyone an equal chance to succeed. Older students with the same reading ability very often have varied interests and training. Therefore, plan to give them more than one passage.

The number of passages and the length of each depend on your particular test. Let's assume the whole exam is on reading. Multiple-choice questions can be asked on very short passages of 35 to 75 words. Quite a few of these can be answered in one period. Student level and passage difficulty naturally influence how many can be done.

Usually longer passages will run from 100 to 300 words. This is sufficient since more than one passage will appear on a single test. Selections for less advanced students will run from about 100 to 200 words. Those for more advanced students will generally range from 150 to 300 words. Naturally these are very general guidelines.

Selections with considerable variety, detail, and contrast are easiest to prepare questions on. Normally you will only be able to write roughly three questions per hundred words, or four at the most. More than this usually results in looking at insignificant details. Fewer than this is inefficient. Finally, in order not to give some students a special advantage, use at least three to five passages from different sources.

Students who read fairly well can answer about a question a minute–including the reading of the passage. Slower students and those reading difficult technical material may need almost twice as much time. It is a good idea to try some sample passages in class (of the same length and level of difficulty that you plan to use). This prepares students for the instructions and types of questions on the test, and it helps you decide on how much time to allow. Some students will take all the time you give them, so have the students raise their hand when they have finished the in-class practice test. You can allow time for at least 80 percent to finish.

Plan to use a variety of types of questions on your reading test. One very important type is the *paraphrase*. Look at the following example:

> Karate is a science of unarmed self-defense and counterattack. It is a sort of "weapon in an empty hand." In many U.S. cities thousands of young people are developing their minds as well as their bodies by learning karate.[4]

The key portion that we will use for our paraphrase question is "In many U.S. cities, thousands of young people are . . . learning karate." The paraphrase of this is "Karate is being taught to many young Americans." Every word but "karate" is different. Here is the resulting question:

(5.39) In this passage we learn that karate ____

*A. is being taught to many young Americans.

B. and training for the mind are both being

taught. C. can remove a weapon from someone's hand. D. is used to start a fight.

A second type of question, the *synthesis* item, requires integration of ideas from more than one sentence—sometimes from the entire selection. For example, in one simple story used to test reading comprehension, a lady stops at a restaurant to eat. But she looks confused when it is time to pay her bill. Then she says, "I can't pay the bill. My purse is gone." At this elementary level, students simply have to complete "The lady couldn't pay for her lunch because . . ." by choosing this option: "her purse was lost." In short, they just need to pull together the information found in the two sentences.

For a more advanced example of the synthesis question, we will look at the full version of the "karate" passage:

> Karate is a science of unarmed self-defense and counterattack. It is a sort of "weapon in an empty hand." In many U.S. cities thousands of young people are developing their minds as well as their bodies by learning karate. "I've been taking karate lessons for five years now," says sixteen-year-old Bobby Hamilton of Columbus, Ohio, "and it's great! I find myself doing things that I thought I could never do." Paula Jones has just begun taking karate lessons at her high school in Philadelphia. She feels that she has more self-confidence because of the lessons. "I am more aware of myself," she says. "I already have learned so much about self-control. I know everything in life is not going to be easy. Karate helps prepare me for the times when I'll have to meet my problems face to face."[5]

(5.40) A good title for this selection would be ____.

A. Americans Import a Japanese Sport B. Karate—Weaponless Protection for People of All Ages C. School Children Enjoy a New Kind of Physical Education Class *D. Self-Perfection Through Self-Protection

A third kind of question is the *inference* item. It requires students to see implications in what they read. Here is an example from an English test used in the Middle East:

> [Two men, Gerard and Denys, were traveling in a forest. They had just been forced to kill a large baby bear in self-defense.] Then Gerard heard a sound behind them. It was a strange sound, too, like something heavy, but not hard, rushing over dry leaves. It was a large bear, as big as a horse, running after them a short distance away. As soon as he saw it, Gerard cried out in fear, "The baby bear's mother."

(5.41) The mother bear was probably running because it ___
A. was afraid of Gerard and Denys and wanted to escape. *B. wanted to hurt those who had killed its baby. C. was chasing a horse, a short distance away. D. enjoyed running, like horses and other animals do.

Various kinds of problems need to be avoided when preparing reading tests like these for intermediate and advanced students: (1) Tests at these levels should not ask for words or phrases exactly as they appear in the passage. (2) In addition, they should avoid illogical distractors like those in the following item:

(5.42) **(poor)** In this study, the high divorce rate was caused by ___
A. the great kindness of husbands and wives to each other. *B. heavy drinking by the mate who was working. C. positive relationships of parents and children. D. having lots of money to pay bills with.

(3) They shouldn't be written in such a way that they can be answered from general knowledge:

(5.43) **(poor)** In the article, we learn that Adolf Hitler was ___

A. a Russian spy. B. a French ballet dancer. C. an American baseball player. *D. a German dictator.

After you prepare an important reading test, you could try it out in the following way: Copy down only the questions and multiple-choice options. Then have another teacher's class or a group of your friends volunteer to "take" the test—without the reading passage. Those items that nearly 50 percent or more get right are probably poorly written: Examinees may be depending mostly on logic or general knowledge. (See discussions of multiple-choice questions in Chapters 2 and 3 for additional cautions in writing multiple-choice questions.)

2. Multiple-Choice Cloze. Some teachers have suggested cloze tests as a way to test reading comprehension, but one limitation is that standard cloze measures overall proficiency. One writer also points up another problem, by using the following illustration. He indicates that although he has never studied Italian, he can get much of the meaning from simple articles in Italian newspapers. But, he says, if any words were deleted from an article written in Italian, he would be quite unable to predict what to put in those blanks. In short, while he has some passive understanding of Italian, he lacks the productive skill that would be required in a standard cloze test. Realizing that many beginning students have a similar problem with English, this writer suggests using a multiple-choice cloze format so that students might rely on their recognition of the needed word.[6] This kind of cloze test is an interesting alternative to the usual kind of reading comprehension item. But why is it included here under *passage* comprehension? The reason is that often several sentences are needed to provide the build-up of information that can point to what is required in a particular slot.

Here is the first part of a multiple-choice cloze. The correct underlined word is to be circled.

(5.44) Is your home safe? Do it/*you/them/each protect your family? Are you safe of/for/with/*from fire or falling? Do you guard against watching/knowing/*eating/sending unsafe food or drinking poison? It perhaps/*is/

always/so important to keep your home safe *and/ since/because/for develop good safety habits.

A test such as this can be prepared rather easily. The best distractors come from student errors. So if possible, give a standard cloze to a class and use as distractors the most frequent incorrect responses.

A variation on the standard cloze has been used in tests prepared by an African ministry of education. There, as in a number of schools where English is taught as a foreign language, a "set books" section is included on important exams: Students read specific novels or collections of technical essays. Formerly, comprehension was checked by essay questions. Wanting more objectivity (but desiring to keep a "productive" type of test), language specialists at the Ministry wrote paraphrases or summaries from the set books. Then a selected-deletion cloze was made from these summaries. (Some students relied heavily on commercial summaries of the plots of these books. Therefore, Ministry of Education cloze materials avoided the prominent matters covered in these plot summaries.) Here are a few lines from an overview of the first part of the novel *The Citadel*:[7]

(5.45) Andrew Manson began his work as a doctor at Drineffy, a coal mining town in Wales. Here he became friends with a doctor named Philip Denney. They both wanted to stop disease ____(1) that people could become well. ____(2) fact, they even blew up a ____ (3) one night to help ____(4) people's health. In Drineffy, Andrew also met Christine Barlow. She became his ____(5) the day he began working in a town called Aberalaw.

Key: (1) so, (2) In, (3) sewer, (4) improve, (5) wife

We can see that items like number 3 (sewer) are virtually impossible to get right without having read the novel. It would be possible to prepare tests with only "recall" items like this: Factual details from the story that could be answered only if one had read the book. This sample is part general proficiency and part reading comprehension. While it is not a multiple-choice cloze, it could be converted to that form. Doing so, however, would increase the chance factor in students getting the "recall" items right.

See the cloze discussion in Chapter 3 (pages 47 to 52) for examples of instructions on taking a cloze test.

Alternate Forms of Passage-Comprehension Items

For teachers who disapprove of multiple-choice tests (which are used almost exclusively in this section) there are alternate passage-comprehension questions that require active rather than simply passive responses. One limitation, however, is that some of these questions test writing even more than they do reading.

Typical objections to multiple-choice tests include the following: 1) They are passive; 2) they expose students to errors; 3) they may indicate that a student who has just guessed on the test is successful. Many other teachers, however, like multiple-choice reading tests since they reflect the receptive nature of reading. The "exposure to error" objection is actually a misconception. The options in a multiple-choice item are simply alternatives. The sentence stem does not contain any errors. And it is not possible to pass an objective test simply by guessing. For a timed test where guessing might be encouraged, use the simple guessing formula explained earlier in this chapter.

1. Sentence-level items. This kind of item has the advantage of being extremely easy to prepare, and questions requiring only simple responses minimize the mixing of writing skills and reading skills.

a. One form of this is simple completion. With reference to the original passage for item 5.45, we might have the following:

(5.46) The two doctors destroyed the sewer because ______.

A possible answer would be "they wanted to improve the health of the people at Drineffy." We would tell them to avoid an answer like "they both wanted to stop disease." This is a direct quote from the passage.

b. Another open-ended item is sentence explanation. With reference to the "Karate" selection, we have the following:

(5.47) In just a sentence, explain what you feel the main point of the passage is. ______________________

Other alternatives require a paragraph or essay response. But these we consider to be writing tests or general proficiency tests.

2. Editing tests. The "editing" test is a kind of cloze test in reverse. Instead of taking words out, we put words in. Usually these are common words used in your textbook. They must *not* be put in at fixed intervals. Usually no more than one word is inserted per clause and never are two words added in succession. The example that follows shows the first part of an editing test. Here words are added randomly, averaging about one in ten. The longest gap between added words is 14; the shortest is 6.

(5.48) The boy was called Abe. He lived read in a cabin on a small farm. Abe lived with his mother and father stores and sister. His clothes were homemade. He didn't even own language a pair of good shoes. But spend he never went hungry or cold. Abe had to work hard on need the farm, but he was happy because wild there was a lot of love in his family.
Key: read, stores, language, spend, need, wild

This test can evaluate comprehension. But a special use is to check reading speed. A special problem in measuring reading speed is being sure that the material has been understood. After having students do a speed-reading check, some teachers give a simple true-false test. Students must have something like 80 percent comprehension for full credit on the speed test. The editing test, however, can give a "built-in" check of comprehension. As they read quickly through the passage, they draw a line through unneeded words. This shows how far they got in their reading and whether they read with understanding. The test can be made easier by putting in less common words. Here is a sample set of directions: "We have added words to this story. They don't make sense. Cross out any you see. (For example: 'The cow over there is automobile eating grass.' Here you would cross out 'automobile.') Never cross out two words together. There are 25 words to cross out."

Advantages of Passage Comprehension

1. This is the most integrative type of reading test.

2. It is objective and easy to score.

3. It can evaluate students at every level of reading development.

Limitations of Passage Comprehension

1. Passage comprehension is more time consuming to take than other kinds of tests.

2. One pitfall in preparing this kind of test is utilizing questions that deal with trivial details.

3. Passage-comprehension tests which use questions on trivial details encourage word-by-word reading.

· ACTIVITIES ·

A. LIMITED RESPONSE. (See pages 76 to 79.)

1. Prepare a list of five pairs of letters that students might confuse. (*Example:* "b" and "d")

2. Prepare a set of ten same-different *phrase* items. Select them from your students' ESL text, or use these phrases and choose five more: at the fountain / has been paid / an ill man / shall we go / that's quite petty. (See item 5.4.)

3. Prepare a set of ten odd-item triplets. Use words from an ESL text. (See item 5.6.)

4. Prepare a set of ten key-word items, each with three distractors, plus the word that matches the key. Select them from your students' ESL text. Or you may use these words and then choose five more: slips, matted, stacks, paper, fright. (See item 5.8.)

B. SENTENCE COMPREHENSION. (See pages 79 to 85.)

1. Prepare or select a set of three related sketches. Prepare a statement on one of them. Make sure it involves reading comprehension. (See item 5.15.)

2. Find a picture—preferably one with various activities in it. Prepare three true-false items related to it. These should be written on a level that your students can understand. Then prepare two yes-no items on the picture. These should be on your students' level. (See item 5.16.)

3. Prepare a list of twenty signs. If these are available in your student text, use them. If not, use signs that your students could encounter in English. Write these out. Then choose five of these to test the meaning of. Prepare five three-option multiple-choice questions that test meaning through paraphrase. (See item 5.28.)

4. Prepare four three-option multiple-choice questions to test the most advanced grammar items that you have recently taught to your students. Or you may use the items below. Use paraphrase. (See item 5.29.)

a. I'd live in a dorm if I didn't have an uncle in town.
b. If she hadn't answered the telephone, she wouldn't have heard the good news.
c. He said I wouldn't graduate unless I studied harder.
d. She'll invite him whether or not he finishes the painting.

5. Prepare sentence-comprehension items. (See item 5.19.)

a. Write five true-false sentences on your students' level.
b. Write directions for these items and include an example.

C. PASSAGE COMPREHENSION. (See pages 85 to 97.) Provide the answer for each test item that you prepare.

1. Prepare eight true-false items on newspaper selections. (See item 5.35.)

a. Find two want ads in a newspaper. They should be on different topics. Write two true-false items on each ad.
b. Find two newspaper articles. Write two true-false items on each article.

2. Read this sample paragraph. Then write multiple-choice distractors for the question below. The question involves implication or inference.

Every line in a drawing is significant. Each one

contributes to the work of the artist. Straight lines dominate drawings of urban streets with tall buildings. What is the reason? Can you guess? City buildings are often austere, cold, and functional. Space in a city is not at all plentiful. Every foot of space is important. Architects plan urban buildings efficiently and economically.[8]

We see in this paragraph that straight lines reflect

_____

*A. the rigidity and economy of city buildings. (See item 5.41.)

3. Find a passage (preferably from an ESL reader used by your students); it should be approximately 200 to 300 words long. Prepare eight to ten multiple-choice questions on the passage. At least four should be paraphrase items, plus two or three items requiring synthesis, and two or three items involving inference. Prepare instructions. (*Examples:* paraphrase [5.39], synthesis [5.40], inference [5.41].)

4. Prepare a multiple-choice cloze test from the following passage. Get three distractors for each word in bold face. If possible, get your distractors by administering the passage to your ESL students or students in another class.

The miller had a hut in a little town in a land across the sea. **The** beautiful castle where the king lived **was** in the same town. But the **miller** had not met the king. One **day** the miller had to take a sack **of** corn to the king's castle. As **he** was going into the castle, he **met** the king. The miller bowed to the **king** and the king stopped **to** talk to him. They talked and **talked.** The miller told the king that he lived in the town. And from this time on, they became the best of friends. (See item 5.44.)

·CHAPTER SIX·

WRITING TESTS

There are many kinds of writing tests. The reason for this is fairly simple: A wide variety of writing tests is needed to test the many kinds of writing tasks that we engage in. For one thing, there are usually distinct stages of instruction in writing, such as pre-writing, guided writing, and free writing. (The *stages* of instruction in writing can be categorized differently from those presented here. See Ann Raimes, *Techniques in Teaching Writing* [in this series] for discussion of *types* of writing and their applications.) Each stage tends to require different types of evaluation. Test variety also stems from the various *applications* of writing. These range from school uses such as note taking and class reports to common personal needs such as letter writing and filling out forms. Besides these, there are specialized advanced applications: the attorney's legal brief or summary, translation, secretarial uses, advertising, research reports, journalism, and literature. Such different writing applications also often call for different test applications.

Another reason for the variety of writing tests in use is the great number of factors that can be evaluated: mechanics (including spelling and punctuation), vocabulary, grammar, appropriate content, diction (or word selection), rhetorical matters of various kinds (organization, cohesion, unity; appropriateness to the audience, topic, and occasion); as well as sophisticated concerns such as logic and style. The list is enough to boggle the mind.

Fortunately we can narrow down the number of tests needed for most ESL classroom purposes. Beginning skills involving penmanship and use of the Roman alphabet can be evaluated informally in class exercises. Very advanced concerns such as evaluating logic and style are beyond the scope of most ESL courses. It is wise to look at writing *applications,* but we will not discuss specialized, advanced matters like translation and evaluating literature. Instead, we will consider more common things like testing letter writing and reports. Our discussion will present techniques for evaluating writing in its various stages, from pre-writing to free writing. The emphasis, however, will be on guided writing including techniques such as dictation.

LIMITED RESPONSE

Techniques for Evaluating Pre-Writing

As we have indicated, formal tests are not needed for teaching the alphabet or cursive writing. Vocabulary and grammar, however, need attention much longer, and so both need to be evaluated. Chapters 2 and 3 can be reviewed in the planning of such tests.

Growing out of grammar instruction are pre-writing activities such as sentence combining, expansion or contraction of sentence elements, copying, and oral cloze. These are only a few of the techniques that can be employed at this stage. The examples that follow illustrate each of these five procedures.

1. Sentence combining, a common pre-writing task, takes many forms. We will look at just two of them: combining by adding a connective and combining by putting one sentence inside the other.

When combining sentences by adding a connective, students can demonstrate their understanding of what various connectives mean—for example, connectives that indicate addition **(and, moreover, furthermore)**, contrast **(but, however, nevertheless)**, and result **(so, consequently, therefore)**. You can provide simple completion contexts that require each one.

(6.1) He likes ice cream <u>but</u> he won't eat any.

(6.2) She didn't feel well today ___so___ she didn't go to work.

(Students will have learned that words like **and** and **moreover** are not always interchangeable.) We can use this approach not only with sentence connectors but also with subordinators—for example, those expressing time **(after, before, since),** condition **(if, whether or not, unless),** and cause **(since, because).**

Combining sentences by having students make internal changes in the grammar also requires considerable proficiency on the part of students. Often the subordinators and conjunctions are provided as in these examples:

(6.3) Some people come late. They will not get good seats. (that)
(*Answer:* People ___that come late will not get good seats___)

(6.4) I am surprised. Nobody likes her. (It ____ that)
(*Answer:* It ___surprises me that nobody likes her.___)

2. Sentence expansion is another kind of pre-writing evaluation. This can involve simply adding words such as adjectives and adverbs. Or it can require adding phrases and clauses.

(6.5) The ( ) man hurried ( ) to the ( ) horse.
(*Answer:* The **old** man hurried **out** to the **frightened** horse.)

(6.6) His decision ( ) surprised everyone ( ).
(*Answer:* His decision **to quit his job** surprised everyone **that knew him.**)

3. Sentence reduction, still another procedure used in evaluating pre-writing proficiency, often provides a cue word (as in the following examples) to show how to begin the new phrase:

(6.7) He told us about a man **who had a wooden leg.** (with)
(*Answer:* He told us about a man **with a wooden leg.**

(6.8) Her father, **who is certainly the stingiest man I know,** wouldn't let us borrow his car. (one word)
(*Answer:* Her **stingy** father wouldn't let us borrow his car.)

Technically, all of the approaches mentioned so far are sentence-level tests. Yet each looks at clause or sentence relationships—an important matter in extended writing. Pre-writing evaluation that extends to several sentences or paragraphs includes the copying task and oral cloze.

4. Copying (sometimes timed) can make students more aware of extended discourse and also of mechanics (especially punctuation and spelling). One type of copying task uses an early audio-lingual technique, the substitution table:

(6.9)

Yesterday,		friends	
Last week,	one of my	teachers	asked me to help
Recently,		brothers	

her		an activity		boys	
him	plan	a party	for the	girls	in our
—		a social		students	

class.	We		finish	
dorm.	The two of us	didn't	get through	until
apartment.	—		stop	

late that evening.		free	
about 6:00 p.m.	If you're	in town	Saturday,
dinner time.		not working	

	join us.
we'd like you to	come too.
	go with us.

Like dictation, discussed later in the chapter, it can be scored by simply deducting one point per error from 100 points.

5. **Oral cloze** combines dictation with selected cloze using high-frequency deletion. Difficult content words or grammar not covered yet can be left intact. Here is part of an oral cloze test. The student hears the text at the left. He reads the part at the right. At each pause, he fills in the missing words. Slashes indicate where pauses would come, for the student to write in the missing words. (See the dictation presentation later in this chapter for details on administering this kind of test.)

(6.10) *(Students hear this)*	*(Students read this)*
Have you ever heard of	Have you ever heard of
Angel Falls?/It's the	Angel Falls? ____ the
highest waterfall/in the	highest waterfall ____
world,/deep in the	the world, deep in ____
jungles/of Venezuela./	jungles ____ Venezuela.
Few people/have ever	____ people ____ ever
seen/Angel Falls. . . .	____ Angel Falls. . . .[1]

Techniques for Evaluating Beginning Writing

In the following sections we will look at a few procedures that can be used with beginning writers. Among the limited-response techniques is the task of simply changing questions to statements, thus "writing" a paragraph. Several multiple-choice items are introduced to test mechanics (such as spelling and capitalization). Easy dictation passages can be given on material such as dialogs that students are already familiar with. Pictures can also be used to cue the writing of short, easy paragraphs. For illustrations of these procedures, see the following sections on guided writing and dictation.

Advantages of Limited-Response Items

1. These are generally quite easy to construct.
2. These are suitable for students with limited ability in English.
3. Except for the open-ended variety, these are rather objective for a writing-related task.

Limitations of Limited-Response Items

1. These do not measure actual writing skill.
2. These can be rather slow to correct—especially the open-ended variety.

GUIDED WRITING

The objective in guided-writing tests is to check student ability to handle controlled or directed writing tasks. One way is to make certain kinds of changes in a story (text manipulation). Another is to expand the outline of an article. Dictation, a third technique, will receive a separate explanation in the next section of the chapter. But before discussing these techniques, we will look at specialized skills tested in writing classes.

Testing Specialized Skills

Specialized areas often evaluated in writing classes include mechanics and larger elements such as unity and organization. Mechanics covers such things as spelling, punctuation, and capitalization.

An old but still acceptable way of checking spelling is to dictate problem words orally. Another way to check spelling is to use a multiple-choice arrangement:

> *Directions:* In each of the following groups of four words, one word is spelled incorrectly; the other three are spelled correctly. Find which word is spelled wrong. Then circle the letter of that word.

(6.11) A. believe B. all right C. because *D. mariage

Unpunctuated sentences such as the following can be used to check both punctuation and capitalization:

(6.12) on december 25 1980 doctor adams died in an automobile accident nevertheless his kind deeds will live on for a long time
(*Answer:* On December 25, 1980, Dr. Adams died in an automobile accident; nevertheless, his kind deeds will live on for a long time.)

Multiple-choice sentences can also be used, but they are slower to prepare, and only one thing can be checked in each item.

Directions: The following sentences contain errors in mechanics. But there are *no* spelling errors. Find the part of the sentence where the mistake occurs. Then circle the letter of that part.

A B C
(6.13) We sent for / a repairman to take / a look at the /
★D
telephone. In the office where I work.

★A B C
(6.14) The Doctor told / the young soldier / to drive south
D
through the valley / for supplies at the nearest city.

In 6.13, the error occurs in part "D"; "in the office where I work" is not a complete sentence; this sentence "fragment" needs to be joined to the main sentence. In 6.14, the error occurs in part "A"; the word "doctor" should not be capitalized unless used with a person's name (Dr. Adams), and then it would be abbreviated.

There are fairly simple ways also to test larger elements like unity and organization. One way is to find a good unified paragraph and then add a sentence that is unrelated. Students have to find the sentence (or sentences) that don't fit. Here is an example:

(6.15) (1) Some people think they have an answer to the troubles of automobile crowding and dirty air in large cities. (2) Their answer is the bicycle, or "bike." (3) In a great many cities, hundreds of people now ride bicycles to work every day. ★(4) Some work with their hands while others depend mostly on their brains while working. (5) A group of New York bike riders claim that if more people rode bicycles to work there would be less dirty air in the city from car engines.[2]

We can use a similar approach to test organization. Find or write a well-organized paragraph with clear transition words. Then scramble the sentences. Students have to put the sentences back into their original order. Here is an example:

(6.16) (1) So on April 18, 1775, he started across the Charles River, where he planned to wait for a signal from a friend. (2) The American Revolution was a citizens' revolution in which ordinary men took a large part. (3) He was living in Boston when British troops arrived to keep people under control. (4) When he saw the lights, he jumped on his horse and rode through the countryside warning the people that they must fight at daybreak. (5) One such man was Paul Revere, a silver worker. (6) Like others, Revere thought the British troops would move from Boston against the villagers. (7) That night after reaching the other side, Revere saw his friend's lantern signals.
(*Key:* 2, 5, 3, 6, 1, 7, 4)[3]

Changing a Passage

Probably no kind of guided-writing test is used more often than that of changing a written passage. The advantage for the student is that he does not have to supply the subject matter. In addition, there are built-in guides to grammatical structure as well.

One technique begins with an artificial paragraph. When the sentences are changed as directed, we have a properly written story. Evaluation concentrates on the grammatical accuracy of the rewritten account. In the example below, the student cues are at the left. At the right we see what the student writes.

(6.17)

(artificial text)	*(student guided-writing test)*
Is it twelve o'clock noon?	It is twelve o'clock noon.
Is Elizabeth sitting in a	Elizabeth is sitting in a
comfortable blue seat?	comfortable blue seat.
Through the window	Through the window
beside her does she see	beside her she sees blue
blue sky and sometimes	sky and sometimes white

white clouds far below?	clouds far below. . .[4]

Another kind of artificial text is one that uses passive sentences. ("The broken typewriter was fixed. Then a letter was typed.") Students are told to change the passive sentences to active and they are given an example of how to begin their "composition": "Anwar fixed the broken typewriter." They continue with, "Then he typed a letter. . . ." Evaluation again concentrates on grammar.

Still another guided-composition test begins with *spoken* English, for example a dialog (MRS. FARIAS: Tell me about Michael. / JOANA: Well, he's very tall.) Students are asked to change this into a narrative, using direct quotations (Mrs. Farias said, "Tell me about Michael." / "Well," replied Joana, "he's very tall.")[5]

If the teacher wishes to test student mastery of indirect speech in writing, he can have a narrative rewritten in this form. Using the example from the previous paragraph, we have:

(6.18) (student guided-writing test)

Mrs. Farias asked her daughter Joana to tell her about Michael. Joana replied that he was very tall. . . .

A typical request in guided-composition testing is to have students make a specific grammatical change: for example, to change the passage from the present continuous to the past, or from the singular to the plural. In the passage below, instructions ask for students to tell this in the third person instead of the first person. The narrator is a girl named Molly:

(6.19) *(original text)*	*(student guided-writing test)*
I was nine when my parents told me they were separating. Even my sister Meghan, then seven, and my brother, Patrick, then four, sensed that something was wrong between our parents. At	**Molly** was nine when **her** parents told **her** they were separating. Even **her** sister, Meghan, then seven, and **her** brother Patrick, then four, sensed that something was wrong between **their** parents.

first, Mom and Dad tried not to argue in front of us, but we saw that they talked to each other less and less.	At first, **their mother and father** tried not to argue in front of **them,** but **the children** saw that **their parents** talked to each other less and less.[6]

Notice that scoring is made easier by having students underline the changes that they have made. When underlining is not practical, you have to decide what to look for. A holistic (general impression) grade can be given, or you can take one point off for specific kinds of errors. (See the discussion on grading at the end of this chapter.)

Building from a Paragraph Outline

One kind of paragraph outline used for testing writing controls the content and the grammar. It takes the following form:

(6.20) I / buy / new white swimsuit / I forget / bring / I / mad / Becky / mother / take / we / shop / Monday night / I find / pretty blue / not expensive. / I start / pay / wallet / gone / I / borrow / money / Becky / mother / I / certainly / upset

The student paragraph might read:

> I bought a new white swimsuit, and then I forgot to bring it. I was really mad. But Becky's mother took us shopping Monday night, and I found a pretty blue one. It was not very expensive. I started to pay for it, and my wallet was gone! I borrowed some money from Becky's mother, but I was certainly upset.[7]

The next form of guided-essay tests relaxes the grammar control a little more, although this particular sample promotes the present perfect tense. Students are to write a paragraph, beginning with this topic sentence: "Several things have contributed to my being an educated person." They are told to consider (but not limit themselves to) the following sentences:

(6.21)
- I have lived in ____ (countries).
- I have traveled in ____ (places).

- I have had certain responsibilities that have matured me. (Name them.)
- I have read _____. (Give an account of reading that has given you special insights.)
- I have talked to _____. (Tell about people from whom you have learned a lot.)
- My parents have taught me _____.[8]

Our final example of a guided-writing test controls the content of the writing but not necessarily the grammar:

(6.22) *Directions:* Write a paragraph of about seventy-five words describing a store or business that you know very well. Base your paragraph on answers to the following questions:

1. What is it called?
2. When did it start to do business?
3. How many employees does it have?
4. What do the employees have to do?
5. Does it have a lot of customers/clients? Why (not)?
6. Why do you choose to go there rather than somewhere else?
7. Is it a good example of what such a store/business should be?

In my neighborhood there is a . . . _____________

(*Note:* These illustrations of guided writing have been drawn from a number of recent ESL texts.)[9]

It is one thing to get students to write. It is quite another matter to grade their writing. As mentioned earlier, you need to decide ahead of time what to evaluate: such as the use of complete sentences, agreement of subject and verb, proper inflections (including tense), and basic mechanics. It is good to limit these to only a few criteria. (See dictation and free composition sections for the discussion on grading.)

Alternate Forms of Guided-Writing Tests

The standard cloze test and the dictation are sometimes also used in a writing class. (See Chapter 3 for a description of the cloze test; the following section discusses dictation.)

Advantages of Guided-Writing Tests

1. Guided-writing tests are rather quick and easy to construct.
2. Because they require an active rather than a passive response, guided testing techniques give the appearance of being an effective measure of writing.
3. Guided-writing tests provide appropriate control for those students who are not ready to write on their own.

Limitations of Guided-Writing Tests

1. Guided-writing tests do not measure ingredients such as organization found in extended writing.
2. Guided writing of the paragraph-outline variety is often rather time consuming and difficult to grade.
3. Guided writing of the paragraph-outline variety is difficult to score with real consistency.

DICTATION

Another guided-writing test is dictation. Most teachers know about this technique, but few handle it properly. Actually, this is one of the easiest tests to use, and it gives very good information on the student's language ability. But this is true only if you prepare it right, present it right, and score it right. You can get good results from a dictation if you follow the steps listed below.

Preparing a Dictation Test

First, choose a story or article that isn't too difficult for your students. You can pick a selection from the reader that you use in class. Even better would be a selection from a reader on a slightly lower level. The length of the dictation depends on whether it is used alone or with other language measures. If it's part of a larger test, you can use a dictation 75 to 100 words long. If it's used by itself, you will want a passage about 125 to 200 words long. (These are of course rather general guidelines.)

Be careful to choose something that is unified and able to stand alone. In order for your students to do their best, they must understand the meaning of the whole thing. You may even want to read your selection ahead of time to a native speaker or to another English teacher to see if he understands it. One way of helping to provide needed unity for a dictation taken from a longer passage is to write an introductory sentence or two. Here you can summarize what preceded the part that you are using. If necessary, you can also add a summary sentence or two at the end.

Unless you're evaluating punctuation, it would be best to avoid a passage with much quoted material in it. Also avoid a passage containing a lot of names and dates and numbers, unless you need to test the ability of students to write out dates and numbers. Of course you can edit or take out a few troublesome words if the passage is suitable otherwise.

After you prepare the modified version, the next step is to decide where the pauses should come. It's here where you will stop for students to write down what they've just heard. Aim for about seven or eight words between pauses, but allow for as few as five and as many as nine or ten words per group. You would very seldom go below five words. Let the structure of the sentence serve as a guide. Longer sentences can be divided between clauses and phrase groups (see the sample dictation). Place a slash (/) at each point that you plan to pause. Be sure to mark the passage in advance–not at the time you're administering the dictation.

If more than one teacher is using the same dictation (and you want to compare the classes), marking the pauses will help make the test more uniform. (See sample dictation 6.23, below.) You should also write out a common set of instructions for the teachers to read aloud to the classes. These directions should be worded simply. For beginning classes in which all students speak the same native language, you can even give the instructions in that language. You can also help to provide uniformity by taping the dictation and by having two teachers score each paper. This is not essential, however.

Administering the Dictation Test

To help students do their best, be sure they know how to take a dictation. You can help assure that they do by giving a practice dictation during the regular class period. When administering dictation as a test, make sure everyone has lined paper and something to write with. Write out on the blackboard any unusual name or expression from the dictation passage that you think could possibly confuse your students. It is also helpful to explain the scoring procedure, if you haven't done this earlier. Then tell them that the dictation will be read aloud three times.

When you read it orally the first time, do not pause during the passage. Students must not write anything at this time. They should simply listen carefully so they can understand what the entire thing is about. The second time, pause after every five to ten words, as previously marked. During each pause, the students are to write down what they have just heard. If they haven't studied much about punctuation yet, you can provide punctuation for them. Do not repeat any words or phrases. Be sure to make your pause long enough so that everyone has time to write down what he has heard. Nothing is gained by having pauses that are very short. In fact, you should watch students to make sure that everyone has had an opportunity to finish writing, before you continue with the next phrase. The third reading, without pauses and at normal speed, provides an opportunity for quick proofreading. But again, no repetition of words or phrases is permitted.

Scoring the Dictation Test

The best way to score a dictation test is to deduct one point for each error. We recommend this even if you are counting off for spelling and punctuation errors. It might seem fairer to take several points off for serious errors and fewer points off for less serious errors. But much practical experience with class dictations has shown this to be time consuming, frustrating, and unreliable. For accurate, fast, reliable scoring, simply take off one point for each error. This includes omitted or added words, inverted word order, grammatical errors—everything. (One exception is to take off one point for the first time a word is misspelled but not for repeated misspelling of the same word. Also, unless there is a need to check student mastery of mechanics, it is all right to ignore errors in punctuation or spelling for beginning to intermediate students.)

An easy way to provide a numerical score for a dictation is simply to give a fixed number of points for it. You can do this regardless of the number of words in the passage. If the dictation is *not* part of a larger test, you can use 100 points. Next, add up the number of errors on each dictation. If no one makes as many as 100 errors, you can just subtract the number of errors from 100 for each person's score. If several students make more than 100 errors, you can divide the number of errors on every paper by 2. You would then subtract this from 100 for their score. (Keep in mind that if many students make numerous errors, you have probably chosen a passage that is too difficult for them. In such a situation, you'll probably want to test them over again using an easier selection.)

If you use dictation and one other measure such as a grammar test or reading comprehension exam, you can allow 50 points for the dictation. Suppose you found papers with the following numbers of errors: 108, 73, 28, 19, and 12. You could divide each by 2 and subtract from 50. The first person would lose 54 points. But since minus scores are not used, he would simply receive 0 on the dictation. (If you wanted to avoid a zero score for the first paper, you could divide the number of errors on all tests by 3 and subtract each of these from 50.)

Let's assume that we need a dictation 75 to 100 words long. At the left (in sample test 6.23) is the first part of a 255-word passage on Norway's fjords. The first two paragraphs combined are about the right length (85 words), but they seem incomplete by themselves. So we add a sentence of our own and begin near the end of the second paragraph.

(6.23) *(original excerpt)*	*(dictation test)*
Have you ever been to Norway? Over a million	Have you ever seen the west coast of Norway? /

people go to see the fjords of Norway every year. Why are these fjords so interesting? Why have people gone back to see them again and again? Let's take a trip to the fjords and see for ourselves.

We'll take a ship to Bergen, in southern Norway, and travel north. The west coast will be on our right. Here we will see steep mountains. The [mountains with their green forests rise right out of the sea.

Narrow arms of the sea reach back into the mountains. We call these narrow arms fjords. If you could see these fjords from the sky, they would look like arms with long fingers. Some are many miles long. Water tumbles into the fjords from waterfalls. There is a narrow strip of level land along the fjords. Here we can see small fishing villages and sometimes a farming village.]

Now our ship is gliding into a fjord. It is

Here mountains with their green forests / rise right out of the sea. / Narrow arms of the sea reach back into the mountains. / We call these narrow arms fjords. / If you could see these fjords from the sky, / they would look like arms with long fingers. / Some are many miles long. / Water tumbles into the fjords from waterfalls. / There is a narrow strip of level land along the fjords. / Here we can see small fishing villages / and sometimes a farming village.
(89 words)[10]

stopping to let us visit a
village. . . .

Advantages of Dictation Tests

1. They can measure general proficiency in English, including many of the integrative skills used in writing.
2. They are easy to prepare.
3. They can be scored with good consistency.
4. They are much harder to cheat on than multiple-choice, completion, or cloze tests.

Limitations of Dictation Tests

1. They are difficult to use for diagnostic purposes. They combine listening and writing.
2. They are not usually helpful in measuring short-term progress.
3. They are not as easy to correct as multiple-choice, completion, or cloze tests.

FREE WRITING

Few teachers have students write without giving them a specific topic. One reason for this is that the skills used in telling a story are quite different from those used in making analogies or refuting arguments. We need to make sure that we're testing what we have taught. Also we need to be certain that each student is performing the same kind of task. Otherwise, we cannot make a fair comparison of their writing. For these reasons, we have to provide clear and rather detailed guidelines for writing—even for advanced students.

Guidelines for Writing Tasks

At upper-intermediate to advanced levels the aim in a writing test is generally to evaluate the effectiveness of the total composition including sentence-level accuracy, larger rhetorical matters such as unity, coherence, and organization, as well as effectiveness in conveying ideas to the intended audience—including socially appropriate language and appropriate selection of supporting details.

While the main aim at advanced stages is not to control grammar, we need to keep in mind that the subject can influence grammatical content: "How to Use a Pay Telephone" will produce the imperative (Pick up the receiver); "A Typical Day at My School" will produce the present tense and expressions of time (in the morning / after lunch). Having students write directions will produce adverbial expressions of place (across from, down, close to). A conversation task will require knowledge of specialized punctuation ("Come in," she said). When preparing a topic for a writing test, we need to be careful, then, to match the assignment to our students' level of training.

It is also good test practice to guide the *content* of what students write. Rarely are we interested in testing creativity, ingenuity, or logic. Guiding the content frees us to look at essentials. One simple way to do this is to use pictures. A travel poster or an advertisement from a magazine can be useful for descriptive writing. A series of pictures (as in some comic strips) can provide guidance for a narrative paragraph.

Another way of controlling content is to provide charts, tables, or diagrams to be explained. With reference to the following lists, students could be told to write a paragraph comparing and contrasting the two cars:

(6.24)	*(your car)*	*(your friend's car)*
horse power	325	220
miles per gallon	16	25
doors	2	4
wheel size	15 inch	15 inch
seating	6	5
fuel used	unleaded	regular
stereo	no	yes
power steering	yes	no
power brakes	yes	yes

Still another way to control content is to provide a situation that determines what students are to write about. The following test item looks at upper-intermediate letter-writing skills:

(6.25) *Directions:* You need a job for the summer. You have just read a "Help Wanted" advertisement for teenage workers (reception, dining room, and cleanup) at the Grand Canyon Lodge in Arizona. Address: U.S. Forest Service, Grand Canyon Lodge, Box 1128, North Rim, Arizona 82117. Write a business letter. Indicate the position applied for. Describe your qualifications, such as your age, language background, travel, and personality characteristics. Indicate when you will be available and how long you can work.

Evaluating Student Writing

The introduction to this chapter pointed out the numerous factors that can be evaluated in a single piece of writing. There are several good reasons why teachers ought to consider limiting the number of factors that they check in compositions, except at the most advanced levels. One reason to evaluate only a few factors at one time is that doing so helps us grade our papers more accurately and consistently. Another reason is to speed up our essay grading. A third reason for limiting the number of factors to be evaluated is to avoid unnecessary discouragement of our students. This latter point deserves elaboration.

Many students are inhibited in their writing because their work has been overcorrected. A more selective grading of writing can offer needed encouragement. Let's illustrate: Suppose you have been working to eliminate fragments ("He went home. Because he finished his work"). Students could be assigned to write a paragraph on a specific topic, in class. In grading this short piece of work, you could look only for fragments. Regardless of other errors, you could give a score of 100 percent to each paper that was free of fragments (and perhaps 75 percent to a paper with one fragment, 50 percent to a paper with two, etc.). Obviously this is not highly efficient, but it is consistent with our handling of spoken English. Students would be tongue-tied if every improper stress, intonation, and trace of foreign pronunciation were corrected. Yet many "conscientious" teachers bloody student writing by red-penciling every error that they can find.

Certainly a compromise between this extreme and the one-item-per-paper scoring would be very natural. Generally, we can look for several items in a given paper. But the number should be rather limited, particularly on the beginning level, and they should always be drawn from concepts that have been covered in class.

There is an extreme to be avoided in the *selective* grading of papers, and that is an exclusive focus on grammar or mechanics. Writing, as we know, is much more than grammar. On the intermediate and advanced levels, we begin to give more attention to rhetorical matters of unity, organization, and coherence, in addition to grammatical accuracy. A test corrected only for grammar—even though written as an essay or letter—is still simply a grammar test. And there are more effective ways to test grammar, as we have seen in Chapter 3. Of course, an occasional focus on grammar or vocabulary or mechanics can have a good "backwash" effect on instruction: Students can appreciate the communicative application of these subskills through classwork.

There are basically two ways to give a formal grade to a piece of writing. One is called *analytical,* and the other *holistic.* Let us take a look at these.

The analytical method attempts to evaluate separately the various components of a piece of writing; it can be illustrated with several approaches. One analytical approach is the "points-off" method. Students begin with 100 points or an *A* grade. Then they lose points or fractions of a grade for errors that occur in their piece of writing. What would we look for in student writing at or below intermediate level? Mechanics might include capitalization (notably at the beginning of sentences), punctuation (especially end punctuation), and spelling (no penalty for more than one misspelling of the same word). Grammar would include basic material that had been taught (at least matters such as sentence sense, verb tense, and word order). A larger element of writing to be included might well be organization. Other possible factors are vocabulary choice and ability to follow the assigned writing task. To avoid failing a student for repeated errors of one kind, it is possible to use the following system: one to two errors = one unit off (for example, *A* to *A*−, or 100 to 95); three to five errors = two units off; and over five = three units off. It is also possible to have grammar errors count double or triple the amount off that mechanical errors do, and for errors in larger elements such as organization to be double the weight of grammar errors.

Another analytical approach reverses the procedure described above. Points are given for acceptable work in each of several areas. Consider the following:

mechanics	20%
vocabulary choice	20%
grammar & usage	30%
organization	30%
TOTAL	100%

Sometimes a big difference appears between the message that the student conveys and his mastery of the language. To encourage such students, it is possible to assign a "split grade" (for example *B*+ / *D*). The one at the left can stand for quality of content; the one at the right, accuracy of language use.

A major problem with analytical approaches is that one never knows just how to weight each error or even each area being analyzed. We avoid this difficulty in holistic grading. Also we focus on communication. We are aware of mechanics and grammar, for instance; but we ask ourselves, "How well does this paper communicate?" Minor mechanical errors that interfere very little require very little penalty. In fact, we don't count them. Instead, we might reduce a grade from *A* to *A*− on the basis of a scattering of these errors. The same principle applies to other areas. To develop a "feel" for such grading, we compare one paper with another. The holistic approach doesn't make us feel as secure as we are when we grade a spelling quiz or grammar exam. Nevertheless, it is one of the best ways to evaluate the complex communicative act of writing. Therefore, although the analytical approach has some things to recommend it, the holistic approach is, on the whole, better.

Advantages of Free-Writing Approaches

1. Despite its limitations, this is an important, sound measure of *overall writing ability.*

2. This can have a good effect on instruction: Students will be more motivated to write in and out of class, knowing that their test will be an actual writing task.

3. There is virtually no chance of getting a passing grade on a free-writing test by cheating. (Like other examinations, it would be conducted in the classroom under supervision.)

Limitations of Free-Writing Approaches

1. Grading of free writing tends to lack objectivity and consistency.

2. Free writing is time consuming to grade.

·ACTIVITIES·

A. LIMITED RESPONSE. (See pages 102 to 106.)

1. Prepare ten sentence-combining items that are suitable for your students. Use sentence connectors (not subordinators). Beginning and lower-intermediate students may need a list of connectors to choose from (see items 6.1, 6.2).

2. Prepare a ten-item expansion task. Use sentences from your students' ESL text. Or you may use the following four sentences and then compose six of your own. Indicate where the additions should be placed. Write out suggested answers (see items 6.5, 6.6).

a. One reason is that he hadn't finished school.
b. The scenery is beautiful.
c. Mary's friend injured her foot.
d. The strike inconvenienced everyone.

3. Prepare a ten-item sentence-reduction task. Underline the part of the sentence to be replaced. Add necessary cue words. Then indicate what the revision should be (see items 6.7, 6.8).

4. Select a 100-to-150-word passage, and prepare an oral cloze like that in this chapter (see item 6.10). Write out a set of instructions.

B. GUIDED WRITING. (See pages 106 to 112.)

1. Write a paragraph to check organization (or find one in your students' ESL text). Use clear transition words (such as "a second reason . . ." or "just before noon . . ."). Scramble the sentences, and prepare instructions for the student (see item 6.16).

2. Find a dialog in one of the texts that you are using in your English class. Copy it out, and write instructions for your students to write a narrative from it, not using any quotation marks. Give a short example. Then prepare a model of what you think the students should write (see item 6.18).

3. Use the passage on bicycle riding, item 6.15 (or if you prefer, use a passage from your students' ESL text). Change it so that only the key words are left (as in the "swimsuit" example, item 6.20). Then write instructions on what students are supposed to do in order to create a paragraph from these key words. Give a short example, and then furnish the "completed" version.

4. Now provide a different kind of guided-writing test. After writing out a set of instructions, prepare six or eight questions on a specific topic (such as a sport, a vocation, a city) (see item 6.22). Then prepare a model of what you think the students should write.

C. DICTATION. (See pages 112 to 117.)

1. Here are the number of errors made by five students on a dictation: 17, 81, 50, 28, 40. Since the dictation was used with a reading comprehension test and a short essay, allow only 30 points for the dictation. Convert the error totals to point scores. (A zero score is permissible, but nearly all should be above zero.)

2. Using the Norway dictation (see item 6.23) as a model, select a passage from your students' ESL text for a dictation test. Shorten it and adapt it by composing a suitable introductory sentence or two. Since it is part of a larger test, this dictation should be 85 to 100 words long. Place slashes (/) at the places where you intend to pause.

3. Identify any problems that you see in the following dictation:

There are both advantages / and disadvantages / in visiting Boston / during your Christmas vacation. / It is pretty cold / and uncomfortable then, / and there is some danger / of catching cold. / But there is / the famous Boston Symphony Orchestra / to hear, and there are famous / historical places everywhere. / There is the Old North Church / and there are / famous schools and museums. / Also, there is Bunker Hill. / It is a famous / battleground of the American Revolution.[11]

4. Count the number of errors that you find in the student paper below. Use the Norway dictation (6.23) as a correction key.

Have you ever been the West coat of Norway? Here are mountins with her green . . . rise out of the sea, nar arms of the sea reach to back the mountins. We call those nar arms fjords. If you see these fjords from the sky, they look like arms with long fingers. Some are many miles long. Water . . . into a fjords from water falls. There is a . . . land along the fjords. Here we see small fish and beaches and sometimes a farm with beach.

D. FREE WRITING. (See pages 117 to 122.)

1. Find or draw a picture sequence that tells a story. Write instructions for your students so they can write a narrative based on the pictures.

2. Find a chart or table or diagram for your students to interpret in a free-writing task. Include this with your set of instructions to the students.

3. Provide a very specific situation to serve as a guideline for your student writing. (Look again at the Grand Canyon Lodge example, 6.25).

4. Using a holistic approach, team up with another teacher and grade a set of compositions, if possible at least 10 to 20 of them. Determine your criteria in advance. Report the results of your grading.

ANSWER KEY

C1

dividing by 2, the scores = 21.5, 0, 5, 16, 10

C3

short phrases, illogical division between phrases, too many proper nouns

C4

approximately 29

·CHAPTER SEVEN·

LISTENING TESTS

There are two broad categories of tests that incorporate the listening skill. One group of these aural tests simply uses listening as a tool to evaluate something else. For instance, in the limited-response section of Chapter 2, we learned how beginners' word mastery could be checked by having them listen and respond to simple commands such as "Hand me the chalk." Listening was also used as a means of evaluating low-level proficiency in grammar and pronunciation. But we have also seen listening used to evaluate more advanced integrative skills–by means of a dictation. And in the following chapter on tests of oral production, we will see listening incorporated as an integral part of speaking evaluation.

The present chapter will give attention to the second broad category of tests that utilize listening–those that evaluate proficiency in the listening skill itself, namely listening comprehension. Since listening includes the recognition of words and structures and pronunciation features, the difference between subskill tests using listening as a tool and the integrative listening comprehension test can be blurred at times. But the essential difference is that subskill tests focus on the linguistic components of language, while the comprehension test is concerned with broader communication. Moreover, broader communication is concerned not with the bits and pieces of language but with the exchange of facts and ideas, as well as interpreting the speaker's intentions.

This chapter begins with a variety of ways to test the listening comprehension of beginning students. It then examines the appropriate-response technique, and it concludes with the testing of extended communication.

LIMITED RESPONSE

There are three simple yet effective ways to test the listening skill of beginning adults or children. One involves listening and native-language responses. Another uses listening and picture cues. A third involves listening plus simple task responses.

Native-Language Responses

There is an interesting little quiz that can be used with beginners during their first days of instruction. Suppose you were teaching Spanish speakers, and suppose also that you had friends who spoke German, French, and Arabic. You could tape random sentences or two-line dialogs of English, intermingled with utterances in these three other languages. After each number on their paper, students could indicate in their native language "English" or "other."

For those just slightly more advanced, you could use true-false questions with the true-false options printed in the native language. Classes with mixed language background could simply circle "T" for true and "F" for false. Depending on how much vocabulary they had acquired, students would respond to questions such as the following:

(7.1) Horses can fly. T ⋆F
(7.2) Houses are bigger than people. ⋆T F

Another approach is to have students listen to single utterances, dialogs, or longer material such as lectures. They could then answer questions on this material in their native language. Or you could write multiple-choice questions in their native language. What they hear would of course be in English, but the multiple-choice options that they read would be in their native language. Here is an example:

(7.3) *(students hear in English)*
"How far is it to New York?"
(students read in their native language)
A. No, not far. B. South of Boston. *C. About 200 miles.

Picture Cues

Visuals of various kinds have long been used to test listening comprehension. Although the technique is not limited to beginning students, it is especially useful with beginners: Students do not need to be literate in their second language in order to be tested.

When using a set of three or four related pictures, keep these ideas in mind: There does not have to be a story line relating the pictures to each other. The same set can be used for several questions. You could duplicate them so each student has his own, or you could make a transparency and use an overhead projector to display them to the class. Another possibility is to sketch them on the chalkboard. If students have their own, they can circle objects referred to, or you can have them identify pictures by number. The sample set on page 130 can be followed by this listening comprehension question:

(7.4) "Although their bikes are clean, the two boys are dirty." (Students would select picture number two.)

Questions can be based on a single picture instead of a set of pictures. Those that work best are sketches including a variety of activities which then serve as distractors. Good pictures are sometimes available in ESL texts, but sometimes you will need to produce your own sketches. The picture on page 131 has several things going on. True-false questions such as the following can be given:

(7.5) The goat is being chased across the field by some men. T *F
(7.6) If the boy's not careful, he'll fall out of the tree. *T F

Here are some easier items for beginning students. They use yes-no responses, but could have been written as true-false questions:

(7.7) Is it starting to rain? *yes no

(7.8) Are these people in a city? yes *no

If testing children individually, you could have them point to the action that you describe. For example:

(7.9) In this picture, three people are running. Show me where these three people are.

This item combines the picture cue with the task response, which is discussed next.

Task Responses

As we have seen in earlier chapters, task or activity responses can be handled individually or in a group. When testing individually, you can have students do various things to show how well they understand. For example, tell the student the following:

(7.10) "Stand up, please. And then walk to the door. After you do this, turn on the light. Then before you sit down, put the small book here on the top shelf."

You could give these commands one or two at a time so that the student's memory would not be overloaded. Small children can be asked to play a game, by arranging objects as you tell them to:

(7.11) "Put the ball in the box. Put the storybook on top of the box. Then make a circle around the box with the beads . . ."

Group responses are possible for both children and adults. Children who know the names of colors can use crayons in answering questions. With reference to the countryside picture used with item 7.5, you could tell children to choose a red crayon, for example. Then say,

(7.12) "Draw a circle around the boy who is up in the tree."

A drawing task can be used with young persons or adults. This can be done freehand or with compass and ruler. Here is a sample set of instructions:

(7.13) [*They hear:*] "Draw a square in the middle of your paper. Make each side about 2 inches (5 centimeters) long. [*pause*] Now draw another square, exactly the same size, on the right of the first square. The second square will touch the side of the first square. [*pause*] Next find the line between the two squares. Make it about 1 inch (2½ centimeters) higher. [*pause*] Now connect the top of this new line with the upper-left corner of the first square. [*pause*] And now connect the top of the middle line with the upper-right corner of

the second square. [*pause*] You have drawn a house. Now draw a window in the first square. [*pause*] Finally, draw a door in the second square."

The drawing should look like this:

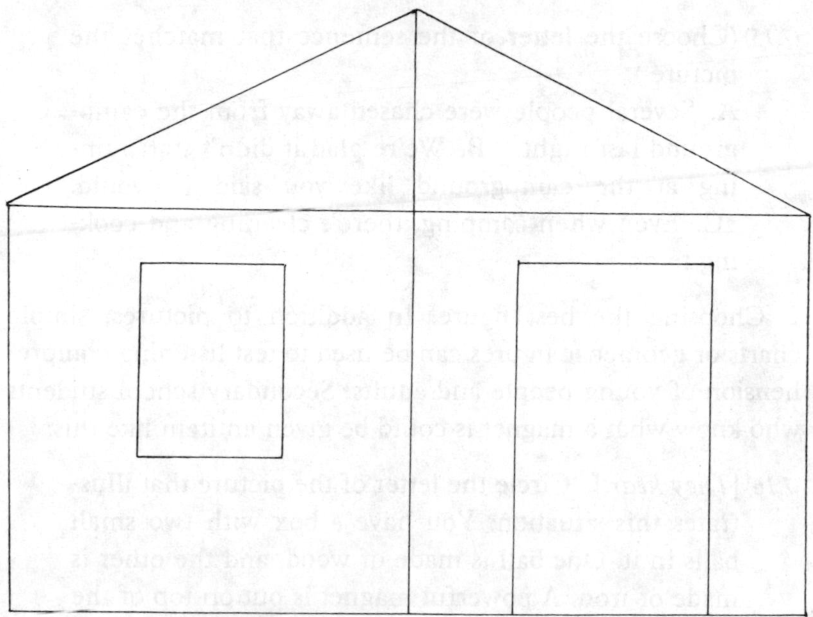

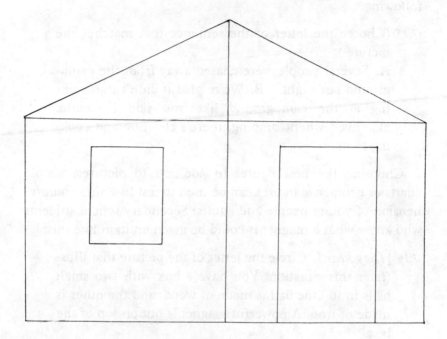

Yet another kind of task response has students trace out directions on a map. Give each person a map (possibly one that you have sketched of the area where they live). Then have them trace directions such as these:

(7.14) [*They hear:*] "You are at the shopping center next to the park. Leave the store opposite the park entrance and walk down Stadium Avenue to the bank. Deposit some money at the bank, and continue along this street past the stadium. Turn right just before reaching the police station and check to see what is playing at the Empire Theater. Now take the shortest route to the post office."

Alternate Forms of Limited Response

1. Choosing the best statement. This time students look at one picture, but they hear three statements. They choose the one that best matches the picture. For example, look again at the picture of the countryside (sample item 7.5). Students would hear the following:

(7.15) (Choose the letter of the sentence that matches the picture.)
A. Several people were chased away from the campground last night. B. We're glad it didn't start raining at the campground like you said it would. ★C. Even when camping, there's cleaning and cooking to do.

2. Choosing the best figure. In addition to pictures, simple charts or geometric figures can be used to test listening comprehension of young people and adults. Secondary school students who know what a magnet is could be given an item like this:

(7.16) [*They hear:*] "Circle the letter of the picture that illustrates this situation: You have a box with two small balls in it. One ball is made of wood, and the other is made of iron. A powerful magnet is put on top of the box."

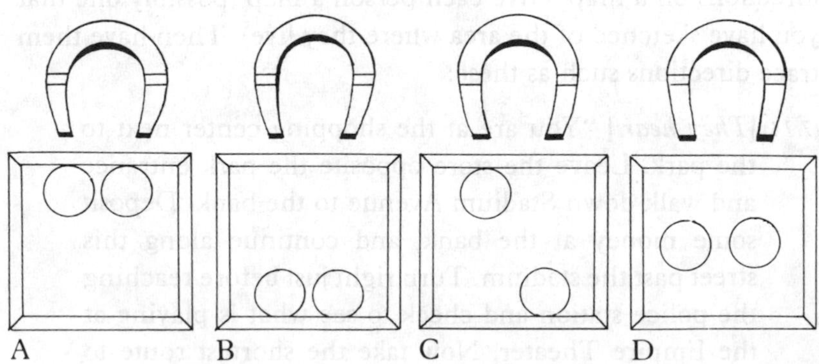

Advantages of Limited Response

1. This is suitable for persons not able to read and write in the target language.
2. This involves flexible techniques: Some are interesting to children, and several techniques are useful for young people and adults with intermediate to advanced skills.
3. The questions are generally quite easy to prepare.
4. Limited-response items are generally rather objective as well as quick and easy to score.

Limitations of Limited Response

1. Native-language responses are limited to classes with bilingual teachers and students with the same language background.
2. Native-language responses are neither needed nor preferred by intermediate to advanced students.
3. Suitable pictures for picture-cue items are not always easy to find.
4. Equipment (such as a Xerox or other copy machine) is usually needed to reproduce drawings for certain task-response and picture-cue items.

MULTIPLE-CHOICE APPROPRIATE RESPONSE

There are three guidelines to keep in mind when preparing multiple-choice appropriate-response items to test listening comprehension: Focus on meaning; keep the options simple; and learn to adjust the difficulty of the items.

1. Focus on meaning. When writing multiple-choice appropriate-response items, use vocabulary and grammar that your students already know. The object is to measure only the students' *understanding* of a particular sentence or short dialog. Look at the following example (the part in parentheses is heard but not read; the three options are read only):

(7.17) (When Jack leaves, they'll hire you, won't they?)
A. Yes, you will. B. Yes, he's leaving. *C. Yes, they will.

The correct reply is "C". Notice that students, in order to answer correctly, have to see what information is directly related to the question, and what is not directly related to it. For example, the question suggests that Jack will leave, but this is not the main point of the inquiry. Therefore, "B" is not appropriate.

Sometimes selecting the best response requires an understanding both of appropriate meaning and appropriate grammar. In 7.18, students have to recognize that the auxiliary verb in the question must also be used in the answer. In 7.19, they have to recognize that different question types take different kinds of answers; and they have to recognize that conversational replies can be given in just a word or a phrase.

(7.18) (Are they coming soon?)
 *A. No, they aren't. B. No, they haven't. C. No, they don't.

(7.19) (Did she buy the old painting or the new one?)
 A. Either one. B. Yes, she did. *C. The old one.

2. Keep the options simple. Look at sample item 7.17 again. Notice how simple and brief the three options are. Each one is only about three words long. Students have to keep the stem in their memory; they won't hear it a second time. Therefore, we use only three options, and we keep these brief so the students won't become confused. Notice, too, that the options are simpler than the stem. In addition, you can see that the distractors are all grammatically correct; they are simply not suitable for this particular context.

3. Learn to adjust the difficulty of the items. We can take items like those illustrated above, and we can make them easier or more difficult. In other words, we can adjust them to match what we have taught our students. Suppose we needed easier questions. We could simplify the stem, and we could make the distractors seem less correct. Let's look at example 7.17 again. We can change the more difficult "hire" to "help" and then shorten the sentence to "Will they help you?" Now change distractor B to "I did." Keep distractors A and C as they are. The result is a much easier question:

(7.20) (Will they help you?)

A. Yes, you will. B. I did. *C. Yes, they will.

There are also interesting ways to make an item more difficult. For example, real-life answers to yes-no questions often drop the yes or no. Let's look at example 7.18 ("Are they coming soon?"). More challenging correct answers would be replies such as "Probably" or "If they have time" or "They haven't said." Now let's take a look at example 7.19 ("Did she buy the old painting or the new one?"). The expected response is "the old one" or "the new one." A less obvious correct answer would be "Neither one." And there's still another way to increase the difficulty of these questions: Change the question to a statement:

(7.21) (She said they're coming here soon.)

*A. How soon? B. They did? C. She is?

Alternate Forms of Multiple-Choice Appropriate Response

There are at least three additional ways to use multiple-choice questions in testing short conversational utterances. None of these uses the appropriate-response technique.

1. One of these is the added comment:

(7.22) (Marie isn't coming.)

A. But she has. *B. But she should. C. But she does.

2. Another is the paraphrase:

(7.23) (Bill isn't any heavier than George.)

A. Bill is heavier. B. George is heavier. *C. They weigh about the same.

3. And the third form is the question on a dialog:

(7.24) ("Should I fill it?"

"Yes. And would you also check the oil?"

"OK. I'll see if the tires are up, too."

—*Where are these people?*)

*A. At a gas station. B. At a police station. C. At a department store.

(7.25) ("How much did that taxi driver charge to bring you from the airport?"
"Fifteen dollars. Is that about right?"
"Well, they charge tourists eight or ten dollars, but I make the trip for about five.")
A. He paid about the right price. B. He paid less than usual. *C. He paid too much.

Again, any test that you write should provide examples to avoid confusion. Also the speech should sound natural, and it needs to be spoken at a normal speed. Two speakers (ideally a male and a female) should be used for dialog items. Allow about an eight-to-ten-second pause between questions for students to read the options and mark their answer. Don't repeat any oral cues.

Advantages of Multiple-Choice Appropriate Response

1. It is fast and easy to correct.
2. It can be scored consistently and reliably.
3. It is an integrative, communicative measure of listening.

Limitations of Multiple-Choice Appropriate Response

1. It is more difficult to prepare than tests for beginners.
2. Cheating is fairly easy, unless alternate forms are used.
3. Since the reading of multiple-choice options is required, students need to be literate in English.

TESTING EXTENDED COMMUNICATION

Our survey of listening tests would not be complete without looking at exams of extended oral communication. Students, especially those in college, need to understand talks and lectures. Also, many of our students want to understand movies, radio and TV programs (ranging from advertisements to newscasts and radio drama). And most students need to understand transactions: asking and receiving directions on how to get to school or buying a bus ticket to another city.

Short Lecture Contexts

To prepare a short lecture context (called a "lecturette"), some teachers feel you can simply use a reading test—the teacher just giving the passage orally instead of in written form. But for at least two reasons this is not satisfactory: First of all, readings lack the natural redundancy that people use in talks and lectures (. . . occurring just **before noon** about **11:40 a.m.,** the **morning** after the robbery). Second, they avoid the lecturer's digressions and false starts (He asked . . . uh, he **told** them to be there. And speaking of . . .). One solution is to use tapes of actual lectures. Another is to begin with a reading and build in natural hesitations, rephrasings, little digressions, plus some redundancy.

There are other things to keep in mind, too, when preparing this kind of listening test. Experience has shown that for test purposes, three or four brief (three- to five-minute) lecturettes are more effective than one long lecture. Also, students should be told to take notes on what they listen to. Moreover, like reading comprehension passages, the short lectures should not be biased in favor of one group of students. Nor should they permit anyone to get answers right simply by calling upon logic or general knowledge.

The following sample avoids the "general knowledge" problem. It is based on an imaginary country. Notice the informal lecture style ("general weather picture," "to give these seasons a handle") and the irrelevant aside in the last few sentences.

> Today I'd like to take a look at the general weather picture in Kochen. This ties in with what the Kochenese do for a living, what kind of crops they grow, and things like that.
>
> Like the whole area, Kochen has a monsoon type of climate. So it is a wet tropical region. The word **monsoon** is from an Arabic word meaning season and refers to a wind system that influences large climatic regions and changes its direction seasonally. In Kochen there are hot, wet southwest monsoon winds which bring in the clouds and heavy rains. Then there

are the northeast monsoons which carry warm, dry air from China, which results in clear skies. The warm, dry season runs from November to February and the rainy season is from May to October. Things really begin to warm up in March and April, which is sort of a transition period. So we have three distinct seasons, one of them rather short. To give these seasons a handle, let's call them the dry season, the rainy season, and the hot season. Again this is pretty typical of this whole area and certainly follows the pattern we find in Thailand, for example.

What are the actual temperatures like? The lowest recorded temperature is 55 degrees Fahrenheit, but temperatures during the coldest part of the dry season usually run around 60 to 65 degrees Fahrenheit. At the other end of the scale, the highest temperature ever recorded was 105 degrees Fahrenheit and again this is somewhat extreme. Usually the mercury hits about 100 during the hottest part of the hot season. But, as those of you know who have experienced weather like this, if you get a stretch of four or five days of 100-degree weather you can be pretty miserable. This is especially true if the humidity happens to take a jump. I guess that's all we have time for.[1]

After listening to this brief lecture and taking notes on it, students would answer printed questions like the following:

(7.26) Where is Kochen?
A. In Europe B. In Central America ⋆C. In the Far East.

(7.27) What is the normal range of temperature in Kochen?
⋆A. Close to 40 degrees. B. About 50 degrees. C. Around 60 to 65 degrees.

Naturally we do not ask questions about asides (which good notetakers would ignore).

Social/Business Contexts

In addition to the short lecture, other interesting contexts for listening comprehension questions include radio and TV commercials, excerpts from radio dramas, extended social conversations (including telephone calls), and routine business transactions. If you decide to use a commercial, make sure it is not too subtle for students to understand. Do *not* have students take notes on what they hear, since this would not reflect what they do in actual life. Questions on the commercial might be either simple completion or multiple-choice. They might take this form: (1) Where does the conversation take place? (2) What is being advertised? (3) Why did the woman become angry?

If you decide to use a business transaction, select a situation that is relevant. The following transaction would be appropriate for young people or adults who travel on commercial airlines. Again, students would not take notes.

"Check in here?"
"Yes. Can I see your ticket, please?"
"Here it is. I'm going to L.A."
"Smoking or nonsmoking?"
"Nonsmoking. And can I get an aisle seat?"
"All right. That's 8-D. Put your bag on the scale, please."
"Sure."
"I'll check it straight through. Here's your boarding pass. That'll be Gate A-16. They'll be boarding in about an hour."
"Oh, is it late?"
"About thirty minutes."
"And, uh, is it a breakfast flight?"
"Yes, it is. Have a good day. Next, please."

Here are some typical questions:

(7.28) What time of day is it?
★A. Morning. B. Afternoon. C. Evening.

(7.29) What is the customer doing?

A. Buying an airplane ticket. B. Checking on someone's flight. *C. Checking in at an airline terminal.

Questions on the last two passages in particular avoid small details (such as "What gate number is the customer going to?"). The reason is that the student does not have notes to refer to. In addition, the questions are kept rather short, with fairly simple vocabulary. We don't want to turn the item into a reading comprehension question.

The passage should be spoken at normal speed with contractions and natural-sounding pauses, hesitations, and the like. If used with more than one class, the passage can be recorded to provide uniformity. Of course two or more different speakers must be used for conversation passages. But keep in mind that using taped passages is not essential in testing listening. In fact, a "live" reading is usually easier for students to understand.

If you decide to use tapes, remember that good recordings are very important and good, clear playback equipment is vital. This sounds quite obvious, but many listening tests are seriously weakened by the use of small, cheap tape recorders. Equally bad is the use of a large, echoing hall or a room where outside noise interferes with the spoken passage. In schools where good tape players and reasonably quiet rooms are not available, simply be aware that your test results will not be as reliable as they would be if these conditions could be met.

Alternate Forms of Extended-Communication Tests

1. Examiner voice. Following a dialog, we can introduce a third voice. For example, after an advertisement, the examiner might ask, "Where is this conversation taking place?" The student would then read, (A) At a church, (B) At a restaurant, (C) At home.

2. Sentence completion. A printed sentence-completion item is also acceptable. For example, item 7.29 could be written in this form:

(7.30) During this discussion, the lady . . .

A. bought an airplane ticket. B. checked on someone's flight. *C. checked in at an airline terminal.

3. Open-ended responses. It is possible to provide a spoken question without multiple-choice options. These are easier to write, but they put more of a burden on the student and they complicate scoring. (For example, should we count off for misspelled words, and do we give partial credit for answers that are not fully correct?) But if only simple responses are called for, this is a legitimate alternative to the multiple-choice listening comprehension question. After the airline check-in passage, we would have the following:

(7.31) What time of the day is it? ______________________

Advantages of Extended-Communication Tests

1. These closely approximate real-life communication.
2. These are fast and easy to correct.
3. These can be scored consistently and reliably.

Limitations of Extended-Communication Tests

1. There is a need for students to be able to *read* English.
2. It is rather difficult to find or prepare natural-sounding listening passages.
3. There is a possibility of students cheating on these tests.

· ACTIVITIES ·

A. LIMITED RESPONSE. (See pages 128 to 135.)

1. Write ten true-false sentences (of the "Snow is warm" variety). Use language appropriate for your students. Make six of your questions false (or illogical) and four of them true (or consistent with reality). Scramble these. Circle the appropriate T or F.

2. Select (or draw) a set of related pictures (such as item 7.4). Write five statements about the four pictures that would be appropriate for your students. Each statement should require students to select the picture being referred to. Indicate which pictures (by number) that the students should select.

3. Look at the drawing that follows item 7.13. Then prepare a drawing of your own (it should be an abstract drawing if it is to be used with upper-intermediate to advanced students). Then write out spoken instructions for a group of students that you typically teach, so that they can reproduce it.

4. Prepare a map showing local streets and businesses. Next, in colored ink or colored pencil, trace a route on that map. Then prepare instructions (to be spoken aloud as a test item) which tell your students how to trace that same route on their maps (see item 7.14).

B. MULTIPLE-CHOICE APPROPRIATE RESPONSE. (See pages 135 to 138.)
If any of the following items are not at the right level for your students, you can substitute sentences that are appropriate.

1. Construct multiple-choice appropriate-response options for the oral cues below. (See items 7.17–7.19.)

a. Does she like to swim?
b. Where did they leave the keys?
c. Is he at the beach or in the mountains?
d. Do you know if he wants me to go? (Do not use "yes" or "no" in correct response.)

2. Construct multiple-choice paraphrase options for the oral cues, or write your own oral cues if these are not right for your students. (See item 7.23.)

a. We thought his bus was due at 10:30, but it pulled in half an hour prior to that.
b. Although Helen is intelligent, she's failing history because of her disinterest.

3. Construct short dialogs that suggest the setting indicated by the correct choice (*) in the following items. (See item 7.24.) Then prepare a set of instructions for this "test."

a. A. in a bookstore *B. in a library C. at school
b. *A. in a restaurant B. at home C. on a picnic
c. A. at a football game *B. at a movie C. at a dance
d. A. at home B. in a hospital *C. at a dress shop

C. EXTENDED COMMUNICATION. (See pages 138 to 143.)
1. Tape two radio or TV commercials, or get them from a published source. Prepare a set of oral instructions for the student. Then write out three multiple-choice questions on each commercial. (See items 7.28, 7.29.)

2. Decide on a situation involving an inquiry or a routine transaction, such as a purchase. Prepare the dialog that illustrates such an inquiry or transaction. Then write out four questions related to the dialog. They can be any type discussed in the section on extended-communication tests; but all four must be the same type. Make sure that they are on the level of your students.

·CHAPTER EIGHT·

SPEAKING TESTS

The testing of speaking is widely regarded as the most challenging of all language exams to prepare, administer, and score. For this reason, many people don't even try to measure the speaking skill. They simply don't know where to begin the task of evaluating spoken language. One purpose of this chapter is to remove a good deal of the mystery surrounding speaking tests. Another purpose is to present the most effective classroom approaches available for measuring oral proficiency.

What are some of the reasons why speaking tests seem so challenging? One reason is that the nature of the speaking skill itself is not usually well defined. Understandably then, there is some disagreement on just what criteria to choose in evaluating oral communication. Grammar, vocabulary, and pronunciation are often named as ingredients. But matters such as fluency and appropriateness of expression are usually regarded as equally important. (In an international survey of speaking tests which was carried out by Randall L. Jones and the author, it was found that of 74 exams evaluated, 81 percent measured grammar, 71 percent fluency, 67 percent vocabulary, 66 percent pronunciation, 63 percent appropriateness, and 37 percent other matters.) Still other factors to be identified in oral communication include listening comprehension, correct tone (sadness or fear, for instance), reasoning ability, and such things as initiative in asking for clarification.

Even when a speaking criterion like fluency is widely

agreed upon, there is some question about how to test it. (Do we look for quickness of response, amount of information conveyed per minute, or simply a general impression of fluency?) In brief, the elements of speaking are numerous and not always easy to identify. Also there isn't very wide agreement on how to weight each factor (such as fluency or grammar). Other concerns related to the testing of speaking include how to get students to speak and how to evaluate so many things at once. There is also the practical problem of having to test each student individually.

Yet another complication is the range of oral communication. At the beginning level we find several pre-speaking activities, like pronunciation and vocabulary identification. We can test beginning-level students by using informal evaluation techniques, or we can use suggestions made in the initial chapters of this book, especially Chapter 4, on pronunciation. Therefore, we will not discuss pre-speaking activities in this chapter.

There are of course numerous advanced applications of speaking: Besides its use in professions like teaching, business, and law, there are specialized uses such as spoken translation by simultaneous translators, professional oral reading by radio newscasters, and dramatic roles on television. However, we will not discuss how to test very advanced and specialized students. Few of our students become this proficient, and commercial tests are available for such purposes (see Appendix).

One way that we can simplify the task of evaluating spoken language is to limit the range of speaking activities tested. (It is suggested that teachers be cautious about using formal tests of speaking at very early stages of instruction. Instead, the relatively nonthreatening limited-response measures that follow are recommended.) We will discuss a few of these activities in this chapter, including how to elicit appropriate speech samples and then how to evaluate these samples.

LIMITED RESPONSE

Students with limited speaking skill can be evaluated by using rather controlled testing methods. Three of the most useful ways are through directed responses, questions about pictures, and reading aloud. All of these can produce connected speech, and all three appear in everyday communication.

For maximum benefit from this limited-response section, also read the final section of this chapter, "Scoring Procedures," particularly the portion on "Objectified Scoring."

Directed Response

Some forms of directed-response cues are quite artificial—very close to imitation. For example,

(8.1) **(cue)** "Tell me he went home."

The response would be, "He went home," simply a repetition of the last part of the examiner's sentence. Yet such requests should always be adapted to the student if possible. Thus, to a native Spanish speaker, we might say,

(8.2) **(cue)** "Tell me that you speak Spanish."

Here at least some modification is required in order to get "I speak Spanish." As mentioned in the dictation discussion, greater skill is required to handle longer sentences. So we can introduce a more challenging sentence like this one:

(8.3) **(cue)** "Tell me that you aren't planning to attend summer school English classes in this city next year."

Here, in addition to handling the longer sentence, the student must change the subject and the verb as well as the contraction in "you aren't" to "I'm not." In addition, the sentence needs to keep the normal speed, stress, and rhythm of the original.

A more lifelike situation can be created if you are able to use another person while giving the speaking test. This could be an advanced student, a community volunteer, or another teacher. The volunteer or teacher could also help with the scoring. Now, as in real life, you can have the student give a message to the other person. For instance, you could say,

(8.4) **(cue)** "Tell her I can see her at noon."

More advanced students would be expected to give a socially appropriate message: "Pardon me, Maria. Mr. Nolan says that he can see you at noon today."

There are other ways of telling the student what to say, of course. Some require more creativity on the part of the examinee:

(8.5) "Remind him what time it is." (Excuse me, Mr. Evans. It's now a quarter to twelve.)

(8.6) "Let her know where the principal's office is." (Ma'am, the principal's office is on the right at the end of the hall.)

A related test item is the directed request. Here the student must ask a question:

(8.7) "Ask her what time it is."

Instructions would indicate that appropriate social phrases should be used. Correct answers might vary from "Pardon me. What time is it?" to "Could you tell me the time, please?" Another directed request might be,

(8.8) "See if he can come back later." (Could you come back later, please? or, Would it be possible for you to come back later?)

Still another form of directed request provides more context and demands more student initiative in answering. To respond properly, students would probably need practice with communicative activities such as problem solving. In the following item, the problem that students have to solve is how to make an appropriate excuse.

(8.9) "Your friend here has just brought you one of your jackets. But the color is terrible for what you are wearing. As kindly as possible, get her to bring another jacket instead." (Thanks a lot, Kay. But could you please get my tan jacket instead? I'm afraid it'll be too cool for this red one.)

Picture Cues

As we have seen before, pictures and objects can be used with young children, and with young people or adults who have limited skill in English. One approach is to use simple line drawings, such as cartoons from a newspaper or simple line drawings like the one below. You can then ask questions such as the following:

(8.10) "Tell me about these pictures. What's happening here?"

Correct answers might be, "She's talking on the phone" or "She's working in an office." How we phrase our question can be very important. If we had said, "What is she doing?" we might have had one-word "vocabulary" answers such as "talking" or "working." In connection with the second picture, we might ask,

(8.11) "Where are they?"

We would accept a short-form answer such as "At a barber shop."

Action pictures like the one on the next page allow us to ask several questions. Also we can prepare more than one form of the test. Otherwise students might anticipate our questions. Pointing to the three children at the right, we could ask,

(8.12) "What did they do?"

If necessary, we can cue the response by pointing at the ball. Their answer might be, "They threw the ball." We can build on this by asking,

(8.13) "What do you think is going to happen now?"

Correct answers might be, "It'll hit the newspaper" or "The man will get mad."

More extended speech and transitions can be produced with a picture sequence. We can illustrate what the students are to say by beginning the story ourselves. The tense we use would depend on our students' background. We might begin this way:

(8.14) "Let's use these pictures and tell a story. I'll begin it. A boy named Tom went to the beach. There he took off his clothes. And then he put on his swimming suit. [*Point at the appropriate pictures.*] Now you tell the rest."

Be prepared to provide additional cues where necessary. If they need further help, ask,

(8.15) "When Tom finished swimming, what did he look for?"

When using pictures, it is best to prepare your questions ahead of time. Write them down, and then read them aloud as the student moves through the test. This can improve the quality of your questions, and it can help with the scoring of the test.

Another way to get connected speech is to use a map. For those who can't read very well, a map like the one on page 154 provides visual cues. Have them look at the dotted line and tell where the person went. As in the previous set of questions, you can give them an example by starting the narration yourself:

(8.16) "Let's look at this picture map of a city. These dotted lines show us where a girl named Anna went. I'll tell what she did first. Anna went out of the market and walked across the street to the church. Then she turned left and walked to the corner opposite the park. Now you tell where she went."

Charts and graphs can also be used with mature students who are literate in their second language. Advanced students can simply be told,

(8.17) "Take two minutes to look at this chart on projected population increases for various parts of the world. Then compare areas of similar growth."

Reading Aloud

Testing students by having them read something aloud offers several advantages and some significant disadvantages. This

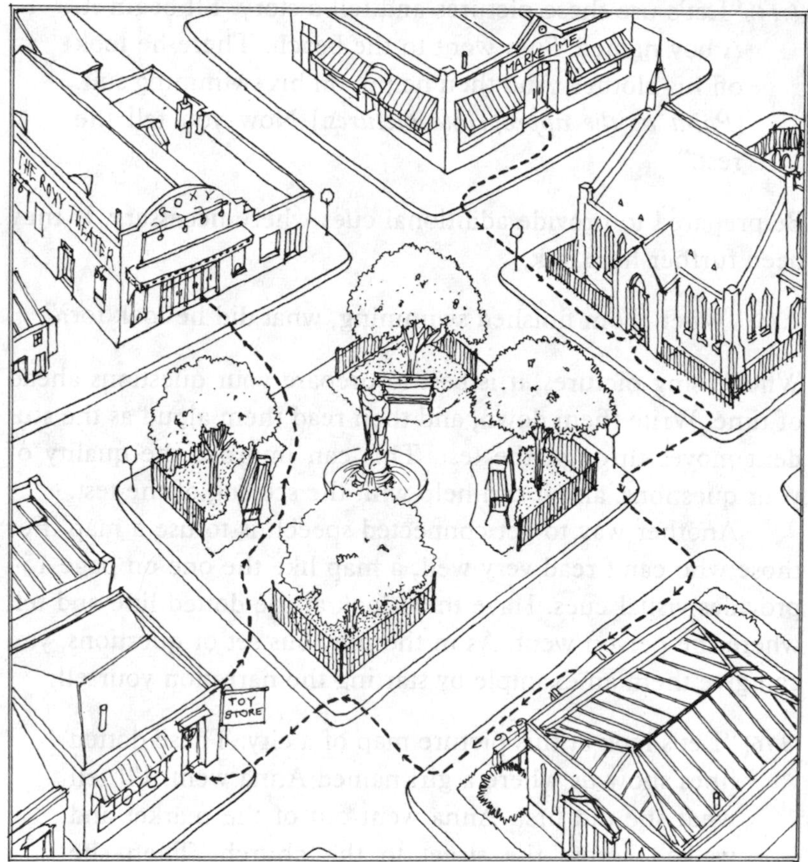

technique provides good control. All students respond in the same way, and so we can make comparisons quite simply. Tests of this kind are generally easy to prepare and to administer, and they avoid our having to find a suitable topic for students to discuss. Besides checking pronunciation, we can see how well our students have mastered the sound-symbol relationships in English. In some programs oral reading is important, and this test technique is obviously a good, direct way to measure oral reading. It can even provide a little help in checking fluency. In addition, reading aloud can give us some idea how well our students have mastered grammar. Like grammatical errors in dictation, errors in reading aloud sometimes reflect confusion about the structure of English.

The limitations of having students read a passage aloud are

equally numerous. Obviously this oral reading technique can't be used with young children who haven't yet learned to read English, or with young people and adults whose speaking skills are much more advanced than their reading skills. Also, there is a tendency for people using the reading-aloud approach to focus almost exclusively on pronunciation. While this is an ingredient in speaking, it is a minor matter at intermediate and advanced levels; pronunciation is certainly not the same as speaking. For one thing, it does not measure interaction skill or appropriateness of response. Finally (as indicated in the chapter on pronunciation), people who have the same skill in speaking often vary a good deal in their ability to read aloud. Native speakers themselves vary considerably in this skill. Yet, recognizing these limitations, we can still occasionally use the reading-aloud procedure.

There are basically two types of reading-aloud tests. One type is a group of sentences that are usually unrelated to each other. The other type is a passage of connected prose. The first permits fairly easy scoring. The second type is more difficult to score, but is often used to diagnose student errors.

The sentences in the first type of reading passages tend to reflect the specific point being tested:

(8.18) He said he didn't care? ↗ [intonation]
(8.19) That's the si<u>xth</u> <u>str</u>iped suit she's sold today. [consonant clusters]

We try to limit ourselves to words students know, so they don't stumble on unfamiliar vocabulary. Also we limit the number of points to look for, anything from one to three being rather typical.

The material for the second type of reading passage could be taken from a reader, possibly a level below the one being studied at the time. It does not have to be very long to give us the information that we need:

(8.20) Not long ago, Josie Evans and her husband Gene were living very much like anyone else. They worked; they drove to town and back on the Los Angeles highways.

> They were busy people. Gene, a cameraman, was making films for television. Josie was selling real estate in the city. But they had their dream, and in 1973, they decided that the time had come to turn that dream into reality. They sold everything they owned—their house, their furniture, and their two cars—and with the money they bought a thirty-two-foot sailing boat. Then they left for a two-year sailing trip . . . covering 10,000 miles in twenty-four months. . . .
>
> The Evanses, who are around fifty and parents of six grown children, sold their boat when they returned. They are now giving lectures to raise enough money for another trip . . . to sail around the world. Their first journey, they agree, has provided the best two years of their lives.[1]

A lower-intermediate selection like the one above could be used with intermediate to advanced students. It takes less than four minutes to read, and it provides a suitable variety of challenges, including well-developed sentences. The scoring of such material will be discussed in the concluding section of the chapter.

Alternate Forms of Limited Response

1. Mimicry. This highly controlled elicitation technique provides an additional advantage to reading aloud: Students can imitate what they hear without having to know how to read. But again, students vary considerably in imitation skills. Moreover, there is no apparent connection between communicative speech and the ability to imitate. In fact, some students with little proficiency can imitate quite well. Mimicry also evaluates other skills at the same time, such as short-term memory and listening.

If you use passages with sentences under 10 or 12 words long, you can simply read a complete sentence aloud and then have the student repeat it.

2. Directed-response role play. Sometimes it is not convenient to have another person present during the exam. Then you can have the student "talk to" someone else in a role-play situation. One way to do this is to borrow a telephone set from the telephone company. The student relays the information that you give him to an imaginary person on the telephone.

3. Variations on visuals. Physical objects, mock-ups (models and cutaway versions ranging from an engine or a piano to a building or the solar system), and student-drawn "maps" of their neighborhood, yard, or living room—these are just a few of the visuals that can be used for students to describe orally.

Advantages of Limited-Response Items

1. These include useful techniques for those with limited language skill (notably directed response and questions about visuals).

2. These provide helpful ways of getting the specific responses that you want.

3. These techniques are generally not threatening. Often the subject matter and even the structure and vocabulary are provided.

4. There is a tendency for these to be interesting and lifelike. Generally they have rather good face validity—that is, they *appear* to measure what they claim to measure.

Limitations of Limited-Response Items

1. Some important features of speaking are not adequately measured, such as fluency and appropriateness.

2. There is not always a direct relationship between speaking proficiency and ability to read aloud or imitate.

3. Student responses are somewhat difficult to evaluate—particularly extended speech (for example, when two or three paragraphs are read aloud).

4. And there are additional difficulties with reading aloud: Some rather fluent students may simply have difficulty with the printed word; also reading aloud is not useful for little children or beginners; finally, there is a tendency to focus exclusively on pronunciation.

GUIDED TECHNIQUES

Less control of spoken utterances is necessary for intermediate to advanced students, but some guidance is needed so that students perform the same kinds of tasks. Consistency in what we have students say helps us to compare their performance over a period of time and to compare the skill of one student with that of another. Some of the techniques already discussed can provide relaxed control. Here is a directed-response item:

(8.21) **(controlled)** "Tell him that it's ten o'clock."
(It's ten o'clock.)

(8.22) **(guided)** "Remind him politely of the time."
(Excuse me, Mr. Evans. It's almost ten o'clock.)

The same contrast can be seen in using visuals. Refer to the beach activity picture accompanying item 8.12.

(8.23) **(controlled)** [*Pointing to the children at the right:*] "What did they just do?"
(They threw a ball.)

(8.24) **(guided)** "Take about a minute and explain some of the main activities in this picture."
(Well, some children are playing with a ball, and it's about to hit a man who is reading a newspaper. And nearby a man is sleeping. . . .)

Besides modifying controlled questions like those above, we can use any of three guided-response techniques: One is the paraphrase; the second is explanation; and the third is guided role play.

But in eliciting speech through guided techniques such as those that follow, we need to recognize that only part of the testing process has been carried out. When eliciting a response, we need to have in mind what it is that we are looking for, such as appropriateness of response, fluency, or linguistic control. As we found in checking pronunciation, it will be profitable to limit the number of factors being evaluated in a given response. After reading this section on guided techniques, you will need to study the final section of this chapter, on scoring procedures, in order to complete the task begun here of evaluating your students' oral communication. (A full-scale discussion on scoring has been brought together at the end of the chapter to avoid duplicating such information on grading by including it after every one of the many elicitation techniques presented in this chapter. Having it in one place also avoids a fragmented presentation of the important issues involved such as holistic and objectified grading. Moreover, it permits readers to make selective use of the elicitation techniques presented and then to make a single convenient reference to appropriate scoring procedures.)

Paraphrase

Paraphrase combines speaking with either listening or reading. Listening plus speaking can be used at almost any level, since students do not need to be literate in English. For example, a teacher of intermediate students might say,

(8.25) "Listen as I read a little story to you about a man and his wife who dreamed of adventure. When I finish, I'd like you to tell me the story in your own words."

The teacher would then read aloud the passage about the couple that sold everything and went sailing (8.20). (See the "Objectified Scoring" discussion on how to approach the scoring of such a passage.)

To save time, teachers with literate students could have pupils read the story silently. In a separate room they would tell their oral paraphrase individually to the teacher. Some teachers like to reduce the memory burden by using simple drawings like those on page 160 to help students recall the details of the story.

Explanation

Explanation and description can be used with students beyond the beginning level. One rather advanced technique is to have students read something silently and then interpret or explain the facts to the teacher orally. This can also apply to a technical

graph, recipe, or math problem that is clearly understood by examinees.

But usually we have students explain something less technical. For example, they can be given two to three minutes to explain how Americans celebrate Thanksgiving, how the British celebrate Boxing Day, or how Moslems observe Ramadan. Obviously the student must be quite familiar with what he is explaining. This is not a culture test. Explanations can also be given of a particular sport such as American baseball or European football, of how to get from one location to another, or of how to do something such as use a pay telephone or a vending machine.

Related to the explanation task is the task of describing something from memory, usually a familiar physical object or location. The object might be a ballpoint pen or a saw, a bicycle or a typewriter. The familiar location might be a bedroom or school playground.

Guided Role Play

Open-ended role play can result in lots of talk from highly imaginative students with outgoing personalities, or it can be unproductive with shy or unimaginative persons. Therefore, we recommend *guided* role play. The teacher or volunteer helper takes a fixed role, and the student responds as prompted. Usually the situation is briefly explained before the role play begins. It is best to have several role plays prepared so that there can be some element of surprise during the discussion. Here is a sample:

(8.26) **Situation:**

There is a "Help Wanted" sign in a supermarket. You are applying for the job. You haven't had a job before. You must talk with the manager. I will be the manager.

TEACHER: Can I help you?
STUDENT: Yes. I want to apply for the job.
TEACHER: I see. We have *two* jobs. One is stacking cans. The other is cleaning.
STUDENT: I want to stack cans.
TEACHER: And why do you prefer that job?
STUDENT: I think it's more interesting.
TEACHER: Have you had any experience?
STUDENT: No, I haven't.
TEACHER: I'll need your name and address.
STUDENT: [*responds with name and address*]
TEACHER: I'm not sure just where that is. Can you tell me how to get there from here?
STUDENT: [*gives directions to his or her home*]
TEACHER: Well, that's all. Call tomorrow afternoon and I'll tell you if you can have the job .
STUDENT: [*thanks the "manager" and turns to leave*]

The teacher or person taking the fixed role should be very familiar with what he is to say. His lines should be spoken at normal speed, and if possible with only an occasional glance at the notes. Also, the person taking the fixed role needs to adapt to what the student says. For instance, one student might begin by saying simply: "My name is Lin." Then the "manager" would have to get the person back on track: "I see. And what can I do for you?"

Advantages of Guided Techniques

1. These allow greater freedom of response than do controlled techniques.
2. These help to get at higher-level matters such as cognitive expression (explanations, for instance) and appropriate response (as in role play).

Limitations of Guided Techniques

1. The most open-ended techniques can be rather difficult to score.
2. Sometimes factors other than speaking ability can interfere with results—factors such as memory, reading ability, and personality. Also, since tests are given individually, sometimes one student helps prepare another student for what to say.

ORAL INTERVIEW

So far we have been looking at ways to get a student to say something in a speaking test. These are called elicitation techniques. Any one of these or a combination of them can be used to test speaking. We now want to consider the oral interview. The interview procedure, however, is not really an elicitation device, but rather a kind of framework for using various elicitation techniques.

Many teachers think of the interview as simply a series of questions and answers. And some amount to no more than that:

(8.27) "What is your name?" (My name is Lin Tan.)
(8.28) "How old are you?" (I'm fifteen years old.) etc.

But the interview can use every elicitation device introduced in this chapter. The whole thing is held together by the constant interaction of the interviewer and the student. This provides an important contrast with other test formats: Instead of simply reciting information, the student is actually talking with someone! The oral interview can provide a genuine sense of communication.

For this reason, rapport is important. Most of us remember being ineffectual on occasion when feeling threatened or talked down to. The good interviewer is neither harsh nor familiar, condescending nor intimidating. A sincere, open, supportive manner is most effective.

Like role play, some direction is needed in order to standardize the test for our students. For this reason a *guided* oral interview is recommended. Your cues for the interview need to be prepared in advance. These you should virtually memorize. Alternate items need to be included so that when students "compare notes" afterwards, the whole procedure does not seem rehearsed. Parts of the interview–especially the initial warm-up–can appear so relaxed that the student may not even be aware that he is being evaluated at that moment. If you know something about the student, you can tailor and personalize the questions. You might begin like this:

(8.29) "Come on in, Tina. Why don't you sit here. Let's see, as I recall you come from Brazil. Sao Paulo?" [You knowingly give the wrong city, and so she has to correct you; she comes from Santos.] (*response*) "Is that a very big place or is it rather small?" (*response*) "Do your parents still live there?" (*response*) "And you're the only member of your family in the United States right now?" (*response*) "Tell me a little about Santos, would you?" (*response*)

Notice that the initial questions are quite simple. In addition, they cover information that the student is thoroughly familiar with. However, they avoid highly personal items: marital status of parents, religion, economic level, weight, age, and "what-did-you-have-for-breakfast" questions. In addition, they include the "truth factor"; that is, they don't ask for manufactured answers ("What time does Mr. Smith wake up in the morning?"/ "At 7:00 o'clock"). They are not language focused ("Change this sentence to the past tense: 'He goes to New York by plane.'") And they are almost exclusively questions that the examiner does not already have the answers to (that is, *not* questions like "What direction do you travel if you fly from New York to London?"/ "You travel east").

A variety of question types is used, especially when testing new students whose skills we are not sure of. Early in the interview, we may ask some yes/no questions.

(8.30) "Do your parents still live there?"

Either/or questions can also be useful:

(8.31) "Is it a large or a small city?"

We have to be flexible in questioning, of course. If the person indicates that he comes from Rio de Janeiro, we wouldn't ask the either/or question on size. Doing so would indicate that the question was artificial (or that the examiner was sadly uninformed).

Incidentally, we have to be careful about the way that we say our either/or questions. If we say, "Do you want to use a pen or a pencil?" the answer would be either "yes" or "no." But if we say, "Do you want to use a pen or a pencil?" the answer would be "a pen" or "a pencil." Normally the latter intonation is what we plan to use. Then a "yes" or "no" answer is clearly incorrect.

Another yes/no item is the statement with question intonation:

(8.32) "You're the only member of your family in the United States?" ↗ (or "Sao Paulo?" ↗)

More demand is placed on the student when we use an information (or wh-) question.

(8.33) "What languages do you speak?"
(8.34) "How long have you been studying English?"

Some questions that look like yes/no items are of course also requests for information.

(8.35) "Would you tell me a little about your home town?" ↘

Appropriate responses to *statements* are still more demanding. It is important when using statements as cues to pause briefly and look at the student as though expecting a response. Otherwise examinees may not feel that any response is needed. Here are some typical statements (without a question tag) that could be used under appropriate circumstances:

(8.36) "It's certainly cold [hot] outside today!" (It surely is.)

(8.37) "Some Brazilians seem to have a hard time adjusting to American food." (Is that so? I haven't had any problem, myself.)

But in providing a variety of elicitation techniques, avoid abrupt shifts in the topic.

One objective in the guided interview is to get the student talking on his own. The use of statements is one way. Another way is providing information that may need qualifying, revising, or correcting.

(8.38) "Is the city of Brasilia in the north or the far south of Brazil?"/(Actually, it's in about the middle of our country.)

(8.39) "I suppose that most Brazilians speak Spanish as well as Portuguese."/(Well, as a matter of fact, not many speak Spanish.)

These kinds of items are used sparingly, of course.

Another way to generate student speech is to mention something or someone needing clarification.

(8.40) "Would you put this on the other teacher's desk after you leave here?" (Pardon me. Which teacher do you mean?)

Items on the guided interview will vary in difficulty, with easier questions coming early. However, after a rather challenging item or two, it is good to insert one or two easy questions. This can help relieve tension and allow the student to regain confidence.

Many responses in a guided interview can be given in just a phrase or a sentence. But several will require extended explanation. The difficulty of these "content" items will vary according to the subject matter and the language of the question. Notice the varying levels of difficulty in these items:

(8.41) "Did you live in a house or an apartment in your country?"

(8.42) "What are the advantages of living in a/an ____ over a/an ____?"

The level of difficulty of items on any given interview should vary both to maintain student confidence and the flow of the interview and also to provide an opportunity for the teacher to see how competent the student really is. For upper-intermediate to advanced students, the interview can be concluded with a challenging item on some contemporary social issue, for example.

Finally, as indicated earlier, the interview should not be limited to just questions (or statements) and responses like those that have been illustrated above. For example, a third person can be involved for role play or relaying information. Visuals and paraphrase techniques can be used. The time spent is also flexible. Some teachers spend as much as fifteen to thirty minutes on an interview. But this is not necessary as a rule. Five to ten minutes per student is generally ample for most classes.

Advantages of the Oral Interview

1. It can be one of the most communicative of all language examinations.
2. It is remarkably flexible in terms of item types that can be included.
3. The scoring tends to be more consistent and simple than the scoring of many guided-technique items.

Limitations of the Oral Interview

1. It is rather time consuming, particularly if taped and scored later.
2. It is deceptively easy for it to become a simple question-and-answer session.

SCORING PROCEDURES

On a speaking test, getting the student to say something appropriate is only half the job. Scoring the test is equally challenging.

In fact, the complex task of scoring a *written composition* is the only thing that matches the challenge of scoring a *speaking test.* Yet there are ways to simplify the scoring. The most successful way is a system of discrete objectified scores for nearly every utterance or response that the student makes. The alternative is to use holistic grading that evaluates the entire body of student speech simultaneously.

The scoring system that we select tends to depend on one of two things: how well trained we are to evaluate oral communication and what factors we choose to evaluate. (Different commercial tests use different approaches to scoring. The well-known Ilyin Oral Interview and the Bilingual Syntax Measure are communicative tests, but both use what we refer to as discrete or objectified scoring procedures. By contrast, the Foreign Service Institute [FSI] Oral Interview uses essentially a holistic approach; FSI examiners have been carefully and extensively trained to administer and score this test.)

Generally speaking, teachers with considerable experience and training (particularly in linguistics and testing) are more inclined to use holistic scoring than teachers without this background. Holistic scoring also tends to be selected when the teacher is inclined toward evaluating a wide variety of criteria simultaneously (such as appropriateness, fluency, grammar, vocabulary, and pronunciation).

Objectified scoring is used both by teachers with little or no specialized training and by highly trained teachers who simply prefer evaluation that is consistent and easy to use.

The main point to be made here is that speaking tests are practical for every ESL teacher to administer and score. Such evaluation happens very naturally in the classroom even during the early weeks and months of instruction. In the primary school classroom, the teacher finds himself reading a story to the children seated around him; he pauses frequently to interact: "Why did Mary run away?" As his pupils respond, he notes whether or not their replies are appropriate and whether communication is interfered with by defective grammar or pronunciation. Almost unaware, he is administering an informal little speaking evaluation as he provides opportunity for speaking practice.

The transition to formal evaluation can be rather simple: The speaking test provides not only a consistent spoken sample of student speech but also a way to *quantify* or score each person's utterance. The discussions that follow on holistic and objectified scoring present two contrasting ways of grading or quantifying student speech.

Holistic Scoring

To understand how the several components of student speech can be evaluated holistically, we will look at examples of holistic scoring procedures used in two commercial speaking tests.

Speaking on the ALIGU Test (see Appendix) has been based for nearly two decades on five criteria: (1) comprehension, (2) pronunciation, (3) grammar and word order, (4) vocabulary, and (5) general speed of speech and sentence length. Each of these is weighted equally. The criteria for grammar and word order follow:

5 points: Uses English with few (if any) noticeable errors of grammar or word order.
4 points: In general uses "good English," but with occasional grammatical or word-order errors which do not, however, obscure meaning (e.g., "I am needing more English").
3 points: Meaning occasionally obscured by grammatical and/or word-order errors.
2 points: Grammatical usage and word-order definitely unsatisfactory; frequently needs to rephrase constructions and/or restricts himself to basic structural patterns (e.g., uses the simple present tense where he should use past or future).
1 point: Errors of grammar and word order make comprehension quite difficult.

0 points: Speech so full of grammatical and word-order errors as to be virtually unintelligible to "the man in the street."

(The points listed above are multiplied by four. Therefore, a top score in all five areas would result in 100 percent or, in other words, native proficiency.) Some sort of scale like this accompanies almost all speaking tests using holistic grading. The examiner listens for all criteria as the interview progresses, sometimes focusing temporarily on one criterion and then another. Sometimes additional questions are asked to clarify a particular area such as vocabulary or comprehension.

Our second commercial test example is the Foreign Service Institute Oral Interview. The highly trained FSI examiners use a dual rating (see Appendix). One is an overall proficiency scale, which describes six functional levels. In addition, examiners fill out a backup checklist used to resolve any differences between the two people evaluating the examinee. The checklist includes ratings on accent, grammar, vocabulary, fluency, and comprehension. But most attention is paid to the functional scale. The six levels range from Level 0 being no proficiency to Level 5 being native proficiency. Level 2 is defined as follows: "Able to satisfy routine social demands and limited work requirements. Can handle with confidence but not with facility most social situations including introductions and casual conversations about current events, as well as work, family, and autobiographical information; can handle limited work requirements, needing help in handling any complications or difficulties; can get the gist of most conversations on nontechnical subjects [i.e., topics which require no specialized knowledge] and has a speaking vocabulary sufficient to express himself simply with some circumlocutions; accent, though often quite faulty, is intelligible; can usually handle elementary constructions quite accurately but does not have thorough or confident control of the grammar."[2]

The advantage of holistic grading is probably obvious: It concentrates on communication while not overlooking the components of speech. The limitation is that a great many teachers (untrained in analyzing speech) find it confusing to evaluate so many things simultaneously. Rating scales have been adapted for the use of teachers, and quite a few teachers have prepared their own. Some experienced ESL instructors in a program with clearly identified evaluation criteria will want to rate their students on a holistic scale. This is unquestionably an ideal rating system, when consistency can be maintained. Yet the vast majority of language teachers do not have the time or opportunity to become expert in using the scales we have discussed. For most teachers, some form of objectified scoring is a practical alternative. (Note that in the chapter on the testing of writing, *holistic* scoring of compositions is recommended, while in this chapter *objectified* scoring of oral interviews is suggested. The main reason for this difference is the assumption that teachers of composition tend to be specially trained to analyze the complexities of writing, a rather advanced skill. But in the area of speaking, the criteria of oral communicative competence are less well defined, and few people have the sophisticated training needed to provide consistent, accurate holistic grading of speech [as carried out on the FSI exam, for instance].)

Objectified Scoring

Items on a quiz or short exam for beginning-level students are sometimes evaluated as being either right or wrong, with no partial credit allowed. For example, on a ten-item test with questions on pictures, we might ask, "What's happening here?" The student looks at a picture of a woman typing and simply says, "She's typing" or "A lady is working." Our evaluation criteria may indicate that any logically appropriate and comprehensible response is acceptable. Here the person gets the item right. But responses like "Yes" or "A lady" or "Working" would receive no credit. What about an answer like, "A lady, she eez working"? The reply is appropriate to the question "What's happening here?" and it is intelligible. Therefore, it is fully correct, despite pronunciation and grammar difficulties.

Other tasks can be handled in a similar way. For instance,

ahead of time, you could divide the route on the picture map into segments. These might correspond to places where the person changes direction or makes a stop. On a twenty-segment map, students would get five points for each part that they describe appropriately, but zero for any part that was incorrect or confusing to the teacher-examiner. A retold story (such as item 8.25) can be divided up into segments and evaluated the same way.

This right-or-wrong arrangement works satisfactorily for some low-level tests. But as teachers we usually feel comfortable with such a scoring system (one allowing no partial credit) only when *we* determine the options, as on a multiple-choice test. Since speaking tests are always productive, we are more satisfied when we can give partial credit. One workable system allows 2 points for fully correct answers, 1 for partially correct responses, and 0 for unacceptable or unintelligible answers. (If there are 25 items on the test, the points could be added up and multiplied by 2, to change this to a percentage.)

When allowing partial credit, be careful not to be too critical of student responses. (Keep in mind that the important FSI interview checklist does not deduct points for accent problems.) If minor pronunciation and grammatical errors are penalized, virtually no one can get a 2 on any item. The result is a 1/0 scoring system, identical to the one discussed initially.

What then should we give partial credit for? This depends of course on our scoring criteria. One suggestion is to give only half credit when serious language errors occur; this includes pronunciation faults that begin to interfere with communication. For example, we have heard "He has a cigarette" pronounced /hiy hæzə síygrət/. The final word sounds so close to "secret" that confusion arises. This sentence would get only half credit, or in other words a "1".

Recall that the ALIGU Oral Rating Form allows 4 out of 5 possible points if occasional grammatical errors (such as "I am needing more English" or "He gave to me the letter") do not obscure meaning. Such sentences could be given 2 points (or full credit) if they were otherwise acceptable. Occasionally, however, a test item focuses on language form, as in a directed request: "Ask him if he wants to go with us." A response like "Are you wanting to go with us?" does not match the language form that we are looking for, even though it doesn't obscure meaning. Under these circumstances, the response would get only half credit. Grammar that is quite mangled ("He wanting go with us?") wouldn't get any points. In brief, when we focus on language in an item, we take off points even for fairly minor errors. Most of the time, however, we give reduced credit for grammar, pronunciation, or vocabulary errors only when they interfere with meaning.

Reduced credit is also given for lack of fluency and for inappropriate utterances. For example, in a role-play test or guided interview, we sometimes find students who need some things repeated; other students are simply very slow in replying, or halting in their speech. For such people, we can give partial credit, even for appropriate and grammatically correct responses. Appropriateness is an important matter, but it doesn't come up quite as often as other criteria. Here is an example: "Ask him politely to wash the car again."/"Wash the car again!" (*Expected request:* "Would you mind washing the car again, please?") The blunt "Wash the car again" would certainly be good for only half credit, even if it were spoken like a native.

For most situations, this partial-credit system works very well, but a minor modification can be helpful on guided interviews and with guided-response techniques. It is possible to give the same amount of credit for each item on the interview (as we do on a dictation). However, content questions with rather open-ended responses (such as "Tell me a little about your home town") are usually more challenging and they anticipate more extended replies than other items (such as "How long have you lived here?"). To reflect this difference in difficulty, you can double their weight. This way, most items count 2 points, while content questions count 4 points (or even 5). You can still use the full-credit/half-credit system, or you can allow 4, 3, 2, 1, or 0 points for content items.

There are three final suggestions on scoring: One is that

even on a speaking test with objectified scoring, it is good to indicate a very general impression of a student's performance. This can be simply an indication that the person is "high," "mid," or "low." The general rating can verify your objectified score. Another suggestion is to use a scoring sheet. At the left you can number the test item. Next to the test number is a short version of your cue ("Tell me about ____"). At the right are at least three boxes for you to check–the first for 2-point answers, the next for 1-point responses, and the next for "0" or unacceptable answers.

The third suggestion is to score the speaking test immediately if possible. This can be done during the exam by another teacher or volunteer that you have trained. Having someone else score allows you to notice gestures and other nonverbal responses that are a part of communication. Generally, however, you will be the only one present other than the student. Therefore, you may want to tape the interview and score it later. The main advantages of this arrangement are that you can concentrate on cueing the student, and you don't make the student nervous by putting a mark down after each utterance that he makes. Usually, however, the scoring of a speaking test is more accurate when it is done *during* the exam. So if you feel comfortable testing and scoring at the same time, we recommend that you handle both together.

Objectified scoring is a perfectly satisfactory way to evaluate speaking tests. But for those interested in learning to score oral tests holistically, the modified system of objectified scoring can be used as a bridge to holistic grading. Initially, all items of an interview can be handled on a 2-1-0 basis. Content questions can later be graded on a 4-3-2-1-0 scale. Later still, guided items or entire speaking tests can be done holistically using a five-point scale. Most ESL teachers, however, can manage quite nicely with the simpler objectified scale.

By utilizing objectified scoring procedures, you can add tests of speaking to the array of communicative and language-skill exams that you are able to prepare, administer, and score. Should the occasion arise that a commercial examination is required, you can consult the Appendix for the test most appropriate for your specific needs.

· ACTIVITIES ·

A. LIMITED RESPONSE. (See pages 148 to 157.)

1. Directed response items.

a. Write instructions and directed-response items that require your students to produce the following sentences. (If these sentences are not appropriate for your students, then write five sentences that *are* suitable. Then follow the directions above.) (See item 8.1 or, for more advanced models, 8.2–8.6.)

(1) She likes you.

(2) The music is too loud.

(3) Thanks very much for showing me the way here.

(4) I wouldn't do that if I were you.

(5) It's quite warm outside today, isn't it?

b. Prepare five directed-request items that require students to produce the sentences below. (Or write five sentences that would be more suitable for your students, and follow the directions above.) (See items 8.7, 8.8.)

(1) When does the game start?

(2) Where is the nearest drinking fountain?

(3) Pardon me, can you speak Spanish?

(4) Could you show me the way to the manager's office, please?

(5) I'm very sorry to be late. (I missed the bus.)

[optional additional explanation]
c. Prepare three situational directed-request items, suitable for your students. (See item 8.9.)

2. Picture-cue items.

a. Find or draw four pictures (like those accompanying items 8.10 and 8.11). Prepare a separate question for each picture; these should be on your students' level. Plan the questions to avoid one-word responses. Give a sample answer for each question.
b. Find or draw a set of pictures that tell a story or incident. Three to five should be enough. Then prepare a question on each frame, to help your students "tell the story." Include the pictures.
c. Prepare or find a map or chart. Write out two questions on this visual; they should be on your students' level. Include the map or chart with your questions.

3. Reading-aloud passage. Select a reading-aloud passage suitable for your students. Include your instructions, and indicate what criteria will be used for grading your students' performance.

B. GUIDED TECHNIQUES. (See pages 158 to 162.)
1. Paraphrase. Select a little story for your students to paraphrase. Write out suitable instructions. (The story is to be read aloud to them.) Provide three or four simple line drawings that can help students recall details from the story.

2. Explanation. Write out five explanation items, such as "Tell how Moslems observe Ramadan." These should be on your students' level. After each item, write out a model explanation.

3. Guided role play. Prepare two guided role plays to test your students with. These should be equal in difficulty. In other words, the same kinds of questions should be asked on each. Only the subject matter should be different. In parentheses, prepare a model student response following each line that the teacher speaks (see item 8.26).

C. ORAL INTERVIEW. (See pages 162 to 166.)
Prepare a 20-item guided oral interview appropriate for your students. Include yes/no, wh-, and either/or questions. Also include statements. Include one or two questions that get the student to offer some kind of correction or modification (see item 8.39). Also include at least one question requiring clarification (see item 8.40). Include at least two or three content questions (see item 8.35). Make sure that most of the questions have some logical relationship to adjoining questions.

D. SCORING PROCEDURES. (See pages 166 to 174.)
Indicate what your evaluation criteria are for the guided oral interview (C above). Also prepare an objectified scoring system for the interview. Administer the guided interview to at least five persons (preferably your students). Using your scoring system, calculate a numerical grade for each person, and report these. Finally, discuss any changes that you would recommend, based on your experience in administering and scoring the guided interview.

·CHAPTER NINE·

EVALUATING TESTS

The previous chapters in this text have discussed how to construct and administer examinations of subskills and communication skills. But one thing more is needed: how to tell whether or not we have been successful—that is, have we produced a good test?

Why is this important? For one thing, good evaluation of our tests can help us measure student skills more accurately. It also shows that we are concerned about those we teach. For example, test analysis can help us remove weak items even before we record the results of the test. This way we don't penalize students because of bad test questions. Students appreciate an extra effort like this, which shows that we are concerned about the quality of our exams. And a better feeling toward our tests can improve class attitude, motivation, and even student performance.

Some insight comes almost intuitively. We feel good about a test if advanced students seem to score high and slower students tend to score low. Sometimes students provide helpful "feedback," mentioning bad questions, as well as questions on material not previously covered in class, and unfamiliar types of test questions.

Besides being on the right level and covering material that has been discussed in class, good tests are also *valid* and *reliable.* A valid test is one that in fact measures what it claims to be measuring. A listening test with written multiple-choice options may lack validity if the printed choices are so difficult to read that the exam actually measures reading comprehension as much as it does listening comprehension. It is least valid for students who are much better at listening than at reading. Similarly, a reading test will lack validity if success on the exam depends on information not provided in the passage—for example, familiarity with British or American culture.

A reliable test is one that produces essentially the same results consistently on different occasions when the conditions of the test remain the same. We noted in Chapter 6, for example, that teachers' grading of essays often lacks consistency or "reliability" since so many matters are being evaluated simultaneously. In defining reliability in this paragraph, we referred to consistent results *when the conditions of the test remain the same.* For example, for consistent results, we would expect the same amount of time to be allowed on each test administration. When a listening test is being administered, we need to make sure that the room is equally free of distracting noises on each occasion. If a guided oral interview were being administered on two occasions, reliability would probably be hampered if the teacher on the first occasion were warm and supportive and the teacher on the second occasion abrupt and unfriendly.

In addition to validity and reliability, we should also be concerned about the *affect* of our test, particularly the extent to which our test causes undue anxiety. Negative affect can be caused by a dictation passage, for example, that is far too difficult, or by an unfamiliar examination task, such as translation if this has not been used in class or on other school exams. There are differences, too, in how students respond to various forms of tests. Where possible, one should utilize test forms that minimize the tension and stress generated by our English language tests.

Besides being concerned about these general matters of validity, reliability, and affect, there are ways that we can improve our tests by taking time to evaluate individual items. While many teachers are too busy to evaluate each item in every test that they give, at least major class tests should be carefully evaluated. The following sections describe how this can be done.

PREPARING AN ITEM ANALYSIS

Selection of appropriate language items is not enough by itself to ensure a good test. Each question needs to function properly; otherwise, it can weaken the exam. Fortunately, there are some rather simple statistical ways of checking individual items. This procedure is called "item analysis." It is most often used with multiple-choice questions. An item analysis tells us basically three things: how difficult each item is, whether or not the question "discriminates" or tells the difference between high and low students, and which distractors are working as they should. An analysis like this is used with any important exam—for example, review tests and tests given at the end of a school term or course.

To prepare for the item analysis, first score all of the tests. Then arrange them in order from the one with the highest score to the one with the lowest. Next, divide the papers into three equal groups: those with the highest scores in one stack and the lowest in another. (The classical procedure is to choose the top 27 percent and the bottom 27 percent of the papers for analysis. But since language classes are usually fairly small, dividing the papers into thirds gives us essentially the same results and allows us to use a few more papers in the analysis.) The middle group can be put aside for awhile. You are now ready to record student responses. This can be done on lined paper as follows:

Item # ____		High Group	Low Group
	A		
	B		
	C		
	D		
(no answer)	(X)		

Circle the letter of the correct answer. Then take the high papers, and start with question number one. Put a mark by the letter that each person chose, and do this for each question on the test. Then do the same in the "Low Group" column for those in the bottom group.

DIFFICULTY LEVEL

You are now ready to find the level of difficulty for each question. This is simply the percentage of students (high and low combined) who got each question right. To get the level of difficulty, follow these steps: (1) Add up the number of high students with the correct answer (to question number one, for example). (2) Then add up the number of low students with the correct answer. (3) Add the sum found in steps 1 and 2, together. (4) Now divide this figure by the total number of test papers in the high and low groups combined. A formula for this would be:

$$\frac{\text{High Correct} + \text{Low Correct}}{\text{Total Number in Sample}} \text{ or } \frac{H_c + L_c}{N}.$$

An example will illustrate how to do this. Let's assume that 30 students (perhaps from two or three classes) took the test. We correct the tests and arrange them in order from high to low. Then we divide them into three stacks. We would have 10 in the high group and 10 in the low group. We set the middle 10 aside. The total number (N) in the sample is therefore 20. We now mark on the sheet how many high students selected A, B, C, or D; and how many low students marked these choices. (If the item is left blank by anyone, we mark the "X" line.) Below is the tally for item 1. Note that "B" is the right answer for this question. We see that 5 in the high group and 2 in the low group got item number 1 correct. Thus $\frac{5+2}{20} = \frac{7}{20} = 35\%$ answered this item correctly.

Item # 1		High Group	Low Group
	A	/	///
	(B)	~~////~~	//
	C	//	/
	D	/	//
(no answer)	(X)	/	//

Now we can see if the item is too easy, too difficult, or "about right." Generally, a test question is considered too easy if more than 90 percent get it right. An item is considered too difficult if fewer than 30 percent get it right. (You can see why by noting that a person might get 25 percent on a four-option test just by guessing.) Referring to the example, we find that item 1 is acceptable. However, it would be best to rewrite much of the test if too many items were in the 30's and 40's.

If you plan to use your test again with another class, don't use items that are too difficult or too easy. Rewrite them or discard them. Two or three very easy items can be placed at the beginning of the test to encourage students. Questions should also be arranged from easy to difficult. Not only is this good psychology, but it also helps those who don't have a chance to finish the test; at least they have a chance to try those items that they are most likely to get right. It is obvious that our sample item would come near the end of the test, since only a third of the students got it right.

Before leaving this discussion of item difficulty, we need to point out that on many language tests (a grammar exam, for instance), it is not completely accurate to think of very difficult and very easy items as "weak" questions. "Difficult" items may simply be grammar points that you have not spent enough class time on or that you have not presented clearly enough. Adjusting your instruction could result in an appropriate level of difficulty for the item. And an easy item simply points up that almost all students in the class have mastered that grammar point. In short, this part of the analysis provides insight into our instruction as well as evaluating the test items themselves.

DISCRIMINATION LEVEL

You can use the same high and low group tally in the previous section to check each item's level of discrimination (that is, how well it differentiates between those with more advanced language skill and those with less skill). Follow these steps to calculate item discrimination: (1) Again find the number in the top group who got the item right. (2) Find the number in the bottom group who got it right. (3) Then subtract the number getting it right in the low group from the number getting it right in the high group. (4) Divide this figure by the total number of papers in the high and low groups combined. A formula for this would be:

$$\frac{\text{High Correct} - \text{Low Correct}}{\text{Total Number in Sample}} \text{ or } \frac{H_c - L_c}{N}.$$

Returning to sample item 1, note that choice "B" is the correct answer. So subtract the 2 persons in the low group getting the item right from the 5 in the high group getting it right. This leaves 3. Dividing 3 by 20, the number of highs plus lows, you get .15, or in other words 15 percent.

Generally it is felt that 10 percent discrimination or less is not acceptable, while 15 percent or higher *is* acceptable. Between 10 and 15 percent is marginal or questionable. Applying this standard to the sample item, we see that it has acceptable discrimination.

There is one caution in applying discrimination to our language tests. When doing an item analysis of rather easy and rather difficult questions, be careful not to judge the items too harshly. For example, when almost 90 percent get an item right, this means that nearly all low students as well as high students have marked the same (correct) option. As a result, there is little opportunity for a difference to show up between the high and low groups. In other words, discrimination is automatically low. Also be careful when evaluating very small classes–for example, those with only 10 or 12 students. This is especially true if students have been grouped according to ability. You can't expect much discrimination on a test if all the students are performing at about the same level. But if you have a number of high and low students, the discrimination figure is very helpful in telling how effective the item is.

When you find items that do not discriminate well or that are too easy or too difficult, you need to look at the language of the question to find the cause. Sometimes you will find negative discrimination–more low students getting a question right than high students. Occasionally even useless items like this can be revised and made acceptable. For example, an evaluation of one overseas test found a question with unacceptable discrimination. Most of the high group thought that the phrase "to various lands and peoples" was wrong; they had learned that "people" did not take the "s" plural, and they did not know this rare correct form. Simply changing this part of the test question resulted in a satisfactory item.

DISTRACTOR EVALUATION

Weak distractors, as we have just seen, often cause test questions to have poor discrimination or an undesirable level of difficulty. No set percentage of responses has been agreed upon, but examiners usually feel uneasy about a distractor that isn't chosen by at least one or two examinees in a sample of 20 to 30 test papers.

But sometimes it does happen that only one or two distractors attract attention. There are three common causes for this: (1) Included sometimes is an item that was drilled heavily in class—an item that almost everyone has mastered. Therefore, the answer is obvious; the distractors cannot "distract." (2) Sometimes a well-recognized pair is used (this/these, is/are, etc.). Even though not everyone has control of these yet, students know that one of the two is the right answer; no other choice seems likely. Here we need to choose another test format. (3) A third cause is the use of obviously impossible distractors: ("Did he do the work?"/*A. Yes, he did. B. Birds eat worms. C. Trains can't fly.).

The tally of student answers also shows how many people skipped each item. Sometimes many questions are left blank near the end of the test. In this case you will need to shorten the test or allow more time for it.

· ACTIVITIES ·

NOTE:
To answer activities 1 to 5 below, do an item analysis on these four multiple-choice questions. There were 27 students in the class, and therefore 9 test papers in each group. (Note in the tallying below that || means 2, and that 𝍸 means 5, etc.)

Item 1

	High	Low
A	//	//
B	/	//
C		
Ⓓ	𝍸 /	////
(X)		/

Item 2

	High	Low
Ⓐ	//	𝍸
B		/
C	𝍸	//
D	/	/
(X)	/	

Item 3

	High	Low
A		//
Ⓑ	𝍸	/
C	/	//
D	///	//
(X)		//

Item 4

	High	Low
A		
B		//
Ⓒ	𝍸 ////	𝍸 //
D		
(X)		

1. Calculate the level of difficulty for each of the four items. Which of these are too difficult, and which are too easy? Submit your calculations with your answer.

2. Calculate the discrimination of each item. Which has the poorest discrimination? Which have unsatisfactory discrimination? Which have borderline? Submit calculations.

3. Look at the distractors in the four items. In which are they the most effective? In which are they the least effective?

4. Do we have any item with negative discrimination? If so, which one?

5. Which item did the fewest students leave blank? Which item did the most leave blank?

6. Challenge item. This was not discussed. But it is also possible to do an item analysis on other kinds of tests in addition to multiple-choice. In a paragraph or two, explain how you could calculate level of difficulty and discrimination on a simple-completion test or cloze test. How could you calculate level of difficulty and discrimination for a dictation?

ANSWER KEY

1. 1 = 56%, 2 = 39%, 3 = 33%, 4 = 89%; none = too difficult and none = too easy
2. 1 = 11%, 2 = negative (no discrimination), 3 = 22%, 4 = 11%; 2 = poorest discrimination and it is unsatisfactory; no other unsatisfactory or borderline items
3. 3 = most effective; 4 = least effective
4. yes; 2 = negative
5. fewest = 4; most = 3
6. Simple completion and cloze = same as multiple-choice unless part credit is given for completion (for this situation see dictation explanation).
Dictation level of difficulty = total points High Group + total points Low Group ÷ total points on dictation × total number in sample.

Dictation discrimination = total points High Group − total points Low Group ÷ total points on dictation × total number in sample.

·APPENDIX·

COMMERCIAL TESTS

ESL teachers sometimes have to answer questions from students and administrators about commercial tests. This appendix describes the most important commercial ESL tests in the United States and Great Britain.

Proficiency tests are used more often than other types of commercial ESL exams. Proficiency tests show overall ability in the language, or they tell us how capable a person is in a specific area (such as speaking). They can also show if a person is ready for certain kinds of schooling or work. Tests of language proficiency can be divided into two broad categories: 1) ESL tests measuring communication or language skills; and 2) bilingual tests that show which of two languages a person is more skilled in.

Achievement (or progress) tests that are published commercially will be of less interest to us than proficiency tests because achievement exams are often prepared to measure progress only in a specific textbook series. Most teachers will want to prepare their own classroom progress tests. As we have seen, the main purpose of this book has been to help teachers write good achievement (or progress) exams.

Commercial *aptitude* tests try to tell us how well a person will do in learning a foreign language. They are usually given before the student even begins to study the second language. Only one or two ESL aptitude tests have ever been published, and these are seldom used.

Since students planning to study in the United States would seldom be interested in British examinations and vice versa, we will present American and British exams separately. Beginning with U.S. exams, we will look at ESL proficiency tests, then bilingual measures, and finally achievement and aptitude tests.

U.S. EXAMINATIONS

ESL Proficiency Tests

Title **Test of English as a Foreign Language (TOEFL)**

Author/ Developer (Sponsor) Educational Testing Service, College Entrance Examination Board, Graduate Record Examinations Board

Source TOEFL, Box 899, Princeton, N.J. 08541

Purpose To indicate English proficiency to colleges and universities (primarily U.S. and Canada) and to government and other agencies for placement of students in universities.

Description Three separately timed sections using 4-choice objective questions: 1) listening comprehension (paraphrase, short dialog between two people, and passage comprehension); 2) structure and written expression (completion and error identification); and 3) reading comprehension and vocabulary.

Sample Item (Instructions have the examinees find which underlined word or phrase is an error. The letter of this answer is marked on an answer sheet.)

At first (*A*) the old woman seemed unwilling to accept (*B*) anything that (*C*) was offered her by my friends and I. (**D*)

[D = unacceptable]

Time Approximately 2 hours (plus 1 hour for administrative details).

Level/Age Advanced (but sometimes used with upper intermediate)/adult.

Availability The TOEFL is not sold to individuals; it is given only on set dates and at approved testing centers (write TOEFL for information).

Title **Michigan Test of English Language Proficiency (MTELP)**

Author/Developer English Language Institute, University of Michigan

Source English Language Institute, Testing and Certification Division, University of Michigan, Ann Arbor, Mich. 48109

Purpose To indicate English proficiency to colleges and universities.

Description A 100-item 3-part objective test: 1) 40 grammar items (sentence completion in 2-line dialog [below]); 2) 40 vocabulary items (contextualized synonym and sentence completion); and 3) 20 reading comprehension items (based on 4 reading passages, each 100 to 350 words long).

Sample Item (Instructions have the examinees choose the word or phrase that best completes the sentence. The letter of that answer is marked on an answer sheet.)

"Is Jack a good student?"
"No, he is ____ in the school."
a) worse b) worst *c) the worst d) bad

Time 75 minutes (plus 15 minutes for instruction, etc.).

Level/Age Advanced (but sometimes used with upper intermediate)/adult.

Availability Schools can buy "released" forms of the MTELP, or persons can take the official MTELP at approved testing centers.

The Michigan battery (used to admit students to universities) includes the MTELP (described above), an impromptu 30-

minute written composition, and a test of aural comprehension. One form of the latter is the **MTAC**–the **Michigan Test of Aural Comprehension;** it consists of a 90-item objective test using appropriate response and paraphrase. Now the 45-item **MLC (Michigan Listening Comprehension Test)** is recommended instead. Overseas, an oral interview is often used in place of the listening test.

Note: The Michigan battery described above will shortly be replaced by the **MELAB—Michigan English Language Assessment Battery.** The MELAB will include a new listening test and will be supplemented by a multiple-choice cloze. (A lower-level test is the **EPT/UM—English Placement Test/University of Michigan.**)

Title	**Comprehensive English Language Test (CELT)**
Author/ Developer	David P. Harris and Leslie A. Palmer
Source	McGraw-Hill Book Company, 1221 Ave. of the Americas, New York, N.Y. 10020
Purpose	To measure English ability of nonnative English speakers in high school, college, or adult programs. Used for placement and for achievement.
Description	Three separate tests: 1) Listening–50 items (20 appropriate responses, 20 paraphrases, 10 short-dialog comprehension); 2) Structure–75 items (completion of 2-line dialog [as on MTELP]); 3) Vocabulary–75 items (35 sentence completion, 40 short definitions with 4-option answers).
Sample Item	to show the way A)greet *B)guide C)guard D) gaze
Time	Listening–40 minutes, Structure–45 minutes, Vocabulary–35 minutes.
Level/Age	Intermediate to advanced/teenage and adult.
Availability	Form A available; Form B unpublished.

Title	**Tests of English as a Second Language of The American Language Institute/Georgetown University (ALI/GU)**

Author/ Developer	American Language Institute, Georgetown University
Purpose	Prepared for the United States Agency for International Development (USAID). Designed for use overseas in rating English proficiency of proposed AID trainees. Used only for ALI placement at Georgetown University and USAID overseas evaluation. No other use is permitted.
Availability	Not available for purchase. (See "Purpose" above.)

Several commercial ESL/EFL tests have been authored or coauthored by Donna Ilyin. They include tests of speaking, structure, reading, and listening. The best known is her easy-to-score oral interview:

Title	**Ilyin Oral Interview Test (IOI)**
Author/ Developer	Donna Ilyin
Source	Newbury House Publishers, Inc., 54 Warehouse Lane, Rowley, Mass. 01969
Purpose	To test the ability of secondary-level and adult students to communicate with content appropriateness and structural accuracy. For placement in upper-elementary school to adult programs, for job placement, and for diagnostic information.
Description	No reading or writing. Tests both comprehension and speaking. Administered one-on-one, all questions based on picture booklet (in 2 forms). Fifty items (30 on short form) from simple to difficult. Picture sequences include clock faces to indicate times of various events. Scored on a 2–1–0 basis.
Sample Items	*(easy)* "What is Bill doing in this picture?" *(difficult)* "If it were yesterday at this time, what would Tom have been doing?"

Time Approximately 20 minutes.

Level/Age Near beginning to fairly advanced/upper elementary school to adult.

Availability Available for purchase.

Other Ilyin proficiency tests include the **Listening Comprehension Picture Test (LCPT)** for basic beginners to high intermediate; the **Listening Comprehension Written Test (LCWT)** for high beginners to advanced; the [Cecilia Doherty, Lauri Lee, Lynn Levy, and Donna Ilyin] **English Language Skills Assessment in a Reading Context (ELSA)** for basic beginners to advanced; and the [Jeanette Best and Donna Ilyin] **Structure Test—English Language (STEL).**

Title **Basic English Skills Test (B.E.S.T.)**

Author/Developer Center for Applied Linguistics

Source Center for Applied Linguistics, P.O. Box 4866, Hampden Station, Baltimore, Md. 21211

Purpose To evaluate elementary listening, speaking, reading, and writing of limited-English adults–for class placement, progress check in survival and pre-vocational classes, and diagnosis.

Description 1) Core section–one-on-one interview on social-survival topics, plus sight-word reading task and simple biodata writing task; 2) Literacy skills section–real-life tasks such as reading want ads and completing job applications.

Sample Items *(easy)* [students hear] "Point to the man's right hand."

(more difficult) [students hear] "The lady in this picture wants to go to the supermarket. She's lost. She doesn't know where to go. What does she ask the man?"

Time Core section–5 to 15 minutes. Literacy skills section–about 45 minutes (group administration possible).

Level/Age Near beginning (limited-English)/adult.
Availability Available for purchase.

Besides the B.E.S.T. test, two other exams that evaluate students with little proficiency in English are the **HELP Test** and the **S.L.O.P.E. Test** (both published by the Alemany Press, P.O. Box 5265, San Francisco, Cal. 94101). The **HELP** (the **Henderson-Moriaty ESL/Literacy Placement Test** by Cindy Henderson and Pia Moriaty) features pre-production, recognition, and production items. The **S.L.O.P.E.** (Ann K. Fathman's **Second Language Oral Production Test**) estimates general oral ability by having students produce specific English grammatical structures; diagnostic scores are also produced on these structures.

Two sets of test batteries evaluate students at various grade levels; one is the **MAC: K-12,** the other, the **OAEP.** Published by Alemany Press, the **MAC: K-12** (the **Maculaitis Assessment Program** by Jean D'Arcy Maculaitis) consists of 6 batteries which span all grades and evaluate oral fluency, pronunciation, writing style, vocabulary, listening, etc., as well as global proficiency. The **OAEP** (**Orientation in American English Placement and Proficiency Test** by Thomas C. Brinson, published by the Institute of Modern Languages, Inc., P.O. Box 1087, Silver Spring, Md. 20910) tests on 6 levels, from grade 9 to adult. The OAEP evaluates listening, speaking, reading, and writing; the written portion takes 50 minutes, the oral 10 to 15 minutes.

The final proficiency test to be described is the important new Interagency Language Roundtable Oral Interview (ILR)—a somewhat modified form of the prestigious FSI Oral Interview. still used by the Foreign Service Institute of the U.S. government. The ILR (as well as the FSI) differs from other tests in that it has no set questions. Although developed to test the foreign language skills of native English speakers, it can be used in an ESL setting.

Title **Interagency Language Roundtable Oral Interview (ILR)**

Author/ Developer	(originally) Foreign Service Institute, Department of State / (presently) Interagency Language Roundtable and ACTFL
Source	Interagency Language Roundtable, Box 9523, Rosslyn Station, Arlington, Va. 22209
Purpose	Originally for American government personnel slated for overseas service (diplomats, Peace Corps, military, etc.). Now used for assessing second-language skills for a variety of government and academic purposes.
Description	One or two examiners conduct face-to-face interview in a relaxed, informal setting. A wide variety of elicitation techniques are used. The final global rating is based on the 6-level functional definitions of performance. Ratings range from 0 to 5, with a + possible from 0 to 4.
Sample Items	Questions range from talk about oneself and one's work to role play and discussion of abstract topics and current events.
Time	10 to 30 minutes.
Level/Age	Adult (but has been used with junior high, high school, and college students).
Availability	Not available for purchase. (For information on non-government testing opportunities and tester training, consult Judith E. Liskin-Gasparro, Educational Testing Service, 20-E, Princeton, N.J. 08541.) FSI Testing Kit (French and Spanish) 1979 available at National Audiovisual Center, General Services Administration, Reference Section, Washington, D.C. 20409.

Bilingual Language-Dominance Tests

There are many kinds of bilingual tests. Some measure language proficiency; others look at matters such as personality, student readiness to read, intelligence, and work interests. Bilingual tests of *language dominance* show which language (usually English and the student's native language) the examinee knows best.

There are three ways to check language dominance. These

are: 1) informal observation, 2) questionnaires on language use in the home, and 3) language (dominance) tests. Questionnaires and tests have been written that give "scores" in all three areas. An example of an informal observation checklist or questionnaire is the **Santa Cruz Language and Language Assessment Informal Teacher Observation Instrument.** An example of the questionnaire on language use in the home is the **HBUE—Home Bilingual Usage Estimate.** This scale helps determine who speaks to whom, how often, and in what language. This section will focus on dominance tests.

Title	**Bilingual Syntax Measure (BSM)**
Author/ Developer	Marina K. Burt, Heidi C. Dulay, Eduardo Hernandez Chavez
Source	The Psychological Corporation, 757 Third Ave., New York, N.Y. 10017
Purpose	To measure dominance or proficiency.
Description	This speaking test is administered one-on-one. Questions are asked about pictures. Comprehension of examiner utterances is implicit, but the focus is on correct syntax; errors in pronunciation and vocabulary, for example, are ignored.
Sample Item	*(Point to a pair of birds);* the examiner says, "What are these?" Plural form is required. Even "Chicken*s*" would be accepted.
Languages	English, Spanish, Italian, Tagalog.
Time	10 to 15 minutes.
Level/Age	Grades K to 2; BSM II covers grades 3 to 12.
Availability	Available for purchase.

While some bilingual tests are designed solely for children, the BINL evaluates both children and adults. It is also used to indicate dominance in 32 languages.

Title	**Basic Inventory of Natural Language (BINL)**
Author/ Developer	Charles H. Herbert, Ph.D.

Source	CHECpoint Systems, Inc., 1520 N. Waterman Ave., San Bernardino, Cal. 92404
Purpose	To determine a student's dominance and language proficiency.
Description	Using 3 techniques (including picture sequences), students tell stories. Administered one-on-one. Ten samples of student speech are recorded. Points are given for fluency (number of words) and sentence (grammatical) complexity.
Sample Item	Storytelling from visuals.
Languages	Offered in 32 languages.
Time	10 minutes.
Level/Age	Grades K to 12 / ages 4 to adult.
Availability	Available for purchase.

Additional well-known dominance measures are listed below:

1. **Crane Oral Dominance Test** (Barbara J. Crane) English/Spanish. Ages 4 to 16. Crane Publishing Co., 1301 Hamilton Ave., Trenton, N.J. 08629
2. **Dos Amigos Verbal Language Scales** (Donald E. Critchlow) English/Spanish. Grades K to 6 (ages 5 to 13). Academic Therapy Publications, 20 Commercial Blvd., Novato, Cal. 94947
3. **MAT-SEA-CAL Oral Proficiency Tests** (Joseph H. Matluck and Betty Mace-Matluck) English/Spanish/Cantonese/Tagalog/Iloano/Mandarin. Grades K to 4. 3903 Bailey Lane, Austin, Tex. 78756 (unverified, 1983)
4. **Pictorial Test of Bilingualism and Language Dominance** (Darwin B. Nelson, Michael Fellner, C. L. Norrell) English/Spanish. Grades K to 2. Stoelting Co., 1350 S. Kostner Ave., Chicago, Ill. 60623

Many dominance tests can also be used as bilingual proficiency tests. The following instrument is listed as a bilingual *proficiency* test:

Del Rio Language Screening Test (Allen S. Toronoto et al.) English/Spanish. Grades K to 2. National Educational Laboratory Publishers, Inc., P.O. Box 1003, Austin, Tex. 78767 (unverified, 1983)

Besides bilingual examinations, there are surveys and interview forms such as the following to determine the student's dominant language:

Home Bilingual Usage Estimate (Rudolph V. Skoczylas) English/Spanish. Grades K to 6. Rudolph V. Skoczylas, 7649 Santa Inez Court, Gilroy, Cal. 95020

Achievement Tests

Since achievement (or progress) tests tend to be related to specific textbooks (and because this text has been devoted to achievement exams), this section will be brief. We will simply illustrate the kinds of instruments that are available. The first test listed below applies to a text series for the elementary school; the second to a series written for young adults and adults. The remaining two are not related to a specific textbook series. Note that some tests, such as the Mini-Check exams, may also be used diagnostically.

1. **English Around the World** (Hosman et al.) Grades 1 to 6. A written group test for each of 6 levels. Scott, Foresman and Co., 1900 E. Lake Ave., Glenview, Ill. 60025 (unverified, 1983)

2. **New English 900 Tests** (Author not listed) Young adult and adult. Four tests per level. Evaluation of listening, vocabulary, reading, writing, and structure. Collier Macmillan International, 866 Third Ave., New York, N.Y. 10022

3. **Ullman Achievement/Placement Test** (Ann Ullman) Two-form test evaluating beginners to intermediate (and sometimes advanced). Alemany Press, P.O. Box 5265, San Francisco, Cal. 94101

4. Mini-Check System: Alemany Press. Basic beginner to advanced. Self-scoring tests.

Miscellaneous Mini-Checks for ESL 100 & 200 (Donna Ilyin and Dorothy Messerschmitt) Beginners. Numbers, vowel contrasts, punctuation, structure, etc.

Listening for Structural Cues with the Mini-Check System (Dorothy Messerschmitt)

Aptitude Tests

Language aptitude tests are designed to predict student success in learning a second language. The most well known of these have been prepared for native English speakers who intend to study a foreign language. They are usually administered before the student receives any instruction in the foreign language. Because the MLAT is available for nonnative speakers, we will look at it in some detail:

Title	**Modern Language Aptitude Test (MLAT)**
Author/ Developer	John B. Carroll and Stanley M. Sapon
Source	The Psychological Corp., 757 Third Ave., New York, N.Y. 10017
Purpose	"Predicts how easily and rapidly students will learn a foreign language in the usual classroom situation."
Description	A series of 5 tape-recorded practice exercises in learning various aspects of languages: 1) number learning (aural); 2) phonetic script (audiovisual); 3) spelling clues; 4) structural understanding of sentences; 5) memorization of new words in exotic language. A short form using 3, 4, and 5 above, is available when playback equipment is not available.
Sample Items	Spelling clues: luv [This sounds like "love," so students should choose "C" as its meaning] A) carry, B) exist, *C) affection, D) wash, E) spy Structure: *Money* is his only object. [Which word functions like *Money?*] Not so many *years ago, most farming* was done by hand. *A B C *D*
Languages	English and French.[1] (English form is for native speakers of English; French form is for native speakers of French.)
Time	1 hour (short form 30 minutes).
Level/Age	Grades 9 to 12, college, adult.
Availability	Available for purchase.

Two additional aptitude tests of interest are the EMLAT and the Pimsleur battery:

1. **Elementary Modern Language Aptitude Test (EMLAT)** (Carroll and Sapon) Grades 3 to 6. English/German. The Psychological Corp. (The EMLAT is no longer described in the catalog of The Psychological Corp., but some copies were in stock at the time of the printing of this text.)
2. **Pimsleur Language Aptitude Battery** (Paul Pimsleur) Grades 6 to 12. For native English speakers. The Psychological Corp.

BRITISH EXAMINATIONS

In the United States, the closest thing to an official "examination body" is Educational Testing Service, cosponsor of the TOEFL. But in Great Britain, there are several widely recognized examination bodies, which provide examinations for nonnative speakers of English. Each organization often provides several levels of tests.[2]

Some of the most important organizations that prepare ESL exams are:

1. The English Language Testing Service (ELTS). Sponsored by the British Council and the University of Cambridge Local Examinations Syndicate.
2. The Royal Society of Arts Examinations Board (RSA).
3. University of Cambridge Local Examinations Syndicate (Cambridge).
4. Association of Recognized English Language Schools Examinations Trust (ARELS).
5. Oxford Delegacy of Local Examinations (Oxford).
6. Joint Matriculation Board (JMB).
7. Associated Examining Board (AEB).
8. University of London.

Instead of being sold, tests prepared by these bodies are given in special testing centers throughout Great Britain and abroad.

Passing lower-level tests shows that a person has enough English skills for certain kinds of employment and training programs. Passing higher-level tests can show that English proficiency is high enough for college or university work. For example, a pass on the Cambridge **CPE** (**Certificate of Proficiency in English** exam) is recognized by British universities as fulfilling the English language entrance requirement–at the **GCE** O Level. The **GCE** (**General Certificate of Education** exam) is widely used for U.K. university admission. Sponsored by institutions such as Oxford, Cambridge, London, and northern universities, it covers a variety of subjects. It should not be confused with the ESL/EFL exams prepared by agencies mentioned above. There are two GCE exams: O Level (Ordinary Level) and A Level (Advanced Level). To be admitted to many British universities, students must receive at least *B* in four subjects at the A level.

Following are key tests prepared by British examining bodies:

Title	**English Language Testing Service Examination**
Sponsor	The British Council English Testing Unit, 10 Spring Gardens, London SW1A 2BN, England (or University of Cambridge Local Examinations Syndicate, Syndicate Buildings, 17 Harvey Road, Cambridge CB1 2EU, England)
Purpose	Admission to educational programs and evaluation of English ability in subject matter areas.
Description	1) General English–reading (sentence paraphrase, cloze, comparison of 2 texts), listening (identifying visuals, dialog, appropriate response, lecture); 2) Subject area English–reading, writing, interview.

Title	**Communicative Use of English as a Foreign Language**
Sponsor	The Royal Society of Arts Examinations Board, John Adam Street, Adelphi, London WC2N 6EZ, England
Purpose	For EFL adult students planning to visit, live, work, or study in Britain.

Description Four tests at 3 levels (basic, intermediate, advanced). Intermediate examples: 1) reading–newspaper reports, telegrams (task oriented); 2) listening–dialog, interview, song, lecture, social; 3) writing–letter, diary, forms; 4) speaking–interview, role play, etc.

Title **Test in English (Overseas)**
Sponsor The Joint Matriculation Board (JMB), Manchester M15 6EU, England
Purpose University entrance test.
Description 1) Written English–3 pieces of connected writing, grammar/vocabulary, reading; 2) Aural English–dialog, instructions, lecture, etc.

Title **Stages of Attainment Scale and Test Battery**
Sponsor The English Language Teaching Development Unit Ltd. (ELTDU), 23 Market Square, Bicester OX6 7BR, England
Purpose To measure language ability in commercial or industrial organizations–*not* an academic entrance examination.
Description 1) Stages A–F–listening and speaking, reading and writing; 2) Stages G and H–listening and speaking, reading and writing.

Title **English for Academic Purposes**
Sponsor The Associated Examining Board (AEB), Wellington House, Aldershot, Hampshire GU11 1BQ, England
Purpose Entrance exam for "further and higher education in the United Kingdom."
Description (almost completed, 1983) Series of module exams in English for academic purposes: e.g., in science, engineering, technology, business, social, and administrative studies.

Title	**Certificate of Proficiency in English (CPE)**
Sponsor	University of Cambridge Local Examinations Syndicate (Cambridge), Syndicate Buildings, 17 Harvey Road, Cambridge CB1 2EU, England
Purpose	U.K. university entrance test (O Level); overseas: sometimes an ESL/EFL teaching credential.
Description	Reading comprehension, composition, usage, listening, speaking.

Additional Cambridge exams include the **Preliminary English Test (PET), First Certificate in English (FCE), Diploma of English Studies (DES), English for Business, English for Science,** and other specialized tests.

Title	**ARELS Oral Examinations (Preliminary, Certificate,** and **Diploma)**
Sponsor	Association of Recognized English Language Schools Examinations Trust (ARELS), 125 High Holborn, London WC1V 6QD, England
Purpose	To measure proficiency in understanding and using spoken English.
Description	Wide variety of formats for testing speaking.

Title	**The Oxford Examination in English as a Foreign Language**
Sponsor	Oxford Delegacy of Local Examinations (Oxford), Ewert Place, Summertown, Oxford OX2 7BZ, England
Purpose	To evaluate practical reading and writing skills of persons planning to study in the U.K.
Description	1) Writing (especially letters and notes); 2) Reading (questionnaires, texts etc.).

For more detailed information on these tests and for additional British ESL/EFL tests, see the Davies and West *Pitman Guide,* or circulars from sponsoring examinations agencies. A commercial test has recently been published by Oxford University Press and is available for purchase.

Title	**Oxford Placement Test (OPT)**
Author/ Developer	David Allan
Source	Oxford University Press, Walton Street, Oxford OX2 6DP, England
Purpose	To measure general English ability of nonnative English speakers for school placement on up to 10 levels of proficiency.
Description	A 2-part objectified test: 1) 100 2-choice sentence-completion items (see example–students match printed words with what they hear on a tape); 2) 100 3-choice sentence-completion grammar items.
Sample Item	*(students hear)* "What do you think of the new teachers?" *(students read)* "What do you think of the new / teachers / T-shirts /?" (Students underline the word or phrase that they heard on the tape.)
Time	Part 1–10 minutes, Part 2–50 minutes.
Level/Age	Near beginning to advanced.
Availability	Available for purchase.

·NOTES·

CHAPTER 1

[1]Randall L. Jones, "Testing: A Vital Connection," in June K. Phillips, ed., *The Language Connection: From the Classroom to the World* (Skokie, Illinois: National Textbook Company, 1977) p. 238.

CHAPTER 2

[1]E.C.T. Horniblow and J.J. Sullivan, *The March of Time, Book I, Stories of Long Ago* (Glasgow: The House of Grant, Ltd. 1958) p. 94.

CHAPTER 3

[1]Gladys G. Doty and Janet Ross, *Language and Life in the U.S.A., Volume 1: Communicating in English*, 3d ed. (New York: Harper & Row, Publishers, 1968) p. 73.

[2]John Algeo, *Exercises in Contemporary English* (New York: Harcourt Brace Jovanovich, 1974) p. 113.

[3]Adapted from Jean Praninskas, *Rapid Review of English Grammar,* 2d ed. (Englewood Cliffs, N.J.: Prentice-Hall, Inc., 1975) pp. 129, 230.

[4]Adapted from Russell Baker, "From Bing to Elvis," *New York Times,* October 18, 1977.

[5]Adapted from Jack Martin, "Everybody's Jogging," *Nation's Business,* September 1978.

[6]Russell N. Campbell and Maryruth Bracy, *Letters from Roger: Exercises in Communication* (Englewood Cliffs, N.J.: Prentice-Hall, Inc., 1972) p. 7.

CHAPTER 4

[1]Clifford H. Prator, Jr., "Accent Inventory," supplementary material to Clifford H. Prator, Jr. and Betty Wallace Robinett, *Manual of American English Pronunciation,* 3d ed. (New York: Holt, Rinehart and Winston, Inc., 1972) p. 1.

CHAPTER 5

[1]Mary S. Lawrence, *Writing as a Thinking Process* (Ann Arbor: The University of Michigan Press, 1972) p. 85.

[2]Peter S. Lindsay and Alice Steel, *English Comprehension for Technical Students* (London: Macmillan Education Ltd., 1963, 1972) p. 20.

[3]National Council of Teachers of English (NCTE), *English for Today, Book 1: At Home and At School,* 2d ed. (New York: McGraw-Hill Book Company, 1972) p. 216.

[4]Adapted from James M. Hendrickson and Angela Labarca, *The Spice of Life* (New York: Harcourt Brace Jovanovich, Inc., 1979) pp. 99–100.

[5]Ibid.

[6]D. Porter, "Modified Cloze Procedure: A More Valid Reading Test," *English Language Teaching Journal* 30, No. 2 (January 1976): pp. 151–55.

[7]A. J. Cronin, *The Citadel* (Boston: Little, Brown & Co., 1937).

[8]Jewell A. Friend, *Writing English as a Second Language* (Glenview, Illinois: Scott, Foresman and Company, 1971) p. 27.

CHAPTER 6

[1]NCTE, *English for Today, Book Two: The World We Live In,* 2d ed. (New York: McGraw-Hill Book Company, 1973) p. 151.

[2]Adapted from Paul Pimsleur, Donald Berger, and Beverly Pimsleur, *Encounters: A Basic Reader,* 2d ed. (New York: Harcourt Brace Jovanovich, Inc., 1980), p. 38.

[3]Doty and Ross, *Language and Life in the U.S.A.*, p. 234.

[4]Ibid., p. 30.

[5]Mary Hines, ed., *New English 900: Teacher's Book* 2 (New York: Macmillan Publishing Co., Inc., 1978) p. 62.

[6]Adapted from Alexandra Sheedy, "How Can Mom and Dad *Do* This to Me?" *Seventeen Magazine,* August 1977.

[7]Willard D. Sheeler, *Welcome to English, Book 2* (New York: Oxford University Press, 1976) p. 200.

[8]Doty and Ross, p. 194.

[9]William E. Rutherford, *Modern English,* Vol. 1, 2d ed. (New York: Harcourt Brace Jovanovich, 1975) p. 278.

[10]NCTE, *English for Today, Book Two: The World We Live In,* pp. 139–40.

[11]Adapted from Doty and Ross, p. 64.

CHAPTER 7

[1]Ted Plaister, *Developing Listening Comprehension for ESL Students* (Englewood Cliffs, N.J.: Prentice-Hall, Inc., 1976) p. 19.

CHAPTER 8

[1]Adapted from Lucette Rollet Kenan, *Fact and Fancy: A Basic Reader* (New York: Harcourt Brace Jovanovich, Inc., 1979), p. 23.

[2]*Absolute Language Proficiency Ratings,* Foreign Service Institute circular (Washington, D.C.: November 1968).

APPENDIX

[1]Source of MLAT in French: Institute de Recherches, 34 ouest, rue Fleury, Montreal, Quebec H3L 1S9, Canada.

[2]Sources for the presentation on British examinations include:

1) Susan Davies and Richard West, *The Pitman Guide to English Language Examinations for Overseas Candidates* (London: Pitman Education Ltd., 1981) [revised edition due late 1983];

2) English Language Testing Service, *First Report* [and *User Handbook*] (London and Cambridge: University of Cambridge Local Examinations Syndicate and The British Council, 1982);

3) private communication with British test expert Brendon J. Carroll;

4) Lois Arthur, "EFL Exams in Britain Looked at Comparatively," *TESL Reporter* 13:3 (Spring 1980): 53–55;

5) British Council, "Examinations and Tests in English for Speakers of Other Languages" (1976).

Heaviest reliance was placed on the *Pitman Guide* and Brendon Carroll's comments.

INDEX